Culinary Concepts

Culinary Concepts

100 Recipes and Tips for the Home Chef

Judith Baigent, CCP

Photographs by Marty Snortum

Gibbs Smith, Publisher

TO ENRICH AND INSPIRE HUMANKIND

Salt Lake City | Charleston | Santa Fe | Santa Barbara

First Edition
11 10 09 08 07 5 4 3 2 1

Published by
Gibbs Smith, Publisher
P.O. Box 667
Layton, Utah 84041

Orders: 1.800.835.4993
www.gibbs-smith.com

Designed by Debra McQuiston
Printed and bound in Hong Kong

Library of Congress Cataloging-in-Publication Data
Baigent, Judith.
Culinary concepts : an extraordinary cooking school / Judith
Baigent ; Photographs by Marty Snortum.
    p. cm.
  ISBN-13: 978-1-4236-0083-1
  ISBN-10: 1-4236-0083-5
  1. Cookery. I. Title.

TX715.B4825 2007
641.5—dc22
                           2007017708

Metric Conversion Chart

Liquid and Dry Measures

U.S.	Canadian	Australian
¼ teaspoon	1 mL	1 ml
½ teaspoon	2 mL	2 ml
1 teaspoon	5 mL	5 ml
1 Tablespoon	15 mL	20 ml
¼ cup	50 mL	60 ml
⅓ cup	75 mL	80 ml
½ cup	125 mL	125 ml
⅔ cup	150 mL	170 ml
¾ cup	175 mL	190 ml
1 cup	250 mL	250 ml
1 quart	1 liter	1 litre

Temperature Conversion Chart

Fahrenheit	Celsius
250	120
275	140
300	150
325	160
350	180
375	190
400	200
425	220
450	230
475	240
500	260

To my parents, Jack and Hazel Baigent. I miss you.

In my thirteen-hundred-square-foot classroom, we can have up to twenty-four students creating dishes at the same time.

Contents

Our school has no particular style of cooking. Each teaching chef brings his or her own cooking style and specialty, so the recipes have international appeal.

Acknowledgments

For many years people have asked me when I was going to write a Culinary Concepts cookbook. This was always a project that I put on the back burner until Mary Jane McKitis, one of my product reps who also sells for Gibbs Smith, Publisher, asked me if I would be interested in writing this book for them. What a gift Mary Jane gave me. I always work best with a deadline.

First, I want to thank my wonderful staff, many of whom have been with me since I opened. Margaret Hale, my kitchen manager, came by to wish me luck the day I opened. I was swamped with customers and dishes in the kitchen, so I asked for her help. She has run our kitchen with efficiency ever since. Howard Thompson came to Culinary Concepts right out of culinary school. It has been fun to watch him develop into one of our most popular teaching chefs. Today Howard functions additionally as our cooking school manager. Carol Smith, whose sense of humor keeps smiles on all our faces, helps prepare for classes and is our resident bread-baking authority. We have a great team of school support staff, Cynthia Cushing, Karla McMahon, Sally Curd, Sam Fisher, Nick Banagan and Rene Escarcega.

Thank you to the teaching chefs who rotate classes, Marilyn Davison CCP, Suzan Gross, Dolores Fritzsche, Joy Paul CEPC, Nicky Johnson. Our wine enthusiasts, Ron Newman, who did all the wine pairing for the recipes in this book, and Joe Galkin. Kathy Burke came to Culinary Concepts with extensive management and retail experience. With the wonderful support of Cheryl Richards, people are always greeted with a welcoming smile and great service.

In today's technical world, business cannot run smoothly without someone who is computer savvy. Maggie Dearborn puts together our class brochure three times a year and manages our Web site. The expertise of my entire staff makes each class a unique experience.

My daughter Angela Sue Tamsen, with her knowledge of graphics and purchasing, helped me set up the retail side of Culinary Concepts. Angela, I can't thank you enough for your help.

My above-and-beyond thank you goes to Howard, Margaret, her twin sister, Janet, and my dear friend Carol Ann Noyes for their time and help in preparing for the photographs in this book.

Thank you to all the members of our volunteer program who donate their time to help with our classes.

Over the past twelve years, the cooking school has gone through three renovations. Dorado Designs excelled in their kitchen design and Interwest and Westar supplied the school with wonderful Wolf and SubZero appliances.

Finally, thank you to every student who has made working at Culinary Concepts so much fun. So many of you signed up to test recipes for me. It is one thing for me to teach a recipe in class where I can instruct and guide a person through the process and another to say, "here is the recipe." I need to know you can make it without me being there. My appreciation goes to these recipe testers: E. Decker Adams, Maureen Adams, Craig Adams, Dixie Agnew, Jay Allen, Pat Alley, Nancy Appell, Sandy Arlt, Carrie Bachtell, Joseph John Bahl, Larry M. Barton, Nancy Barton, Bobbie Behm, Ginny Berkey, Doris Berry, Maureen Bike, Connie Braddock, Mardee

Briscoe, Janet V. Burke, Stacy Butler, Rick Cade, Kathie Cade, Sandal D. Caillet, Karen Carter, Maureen Cashin, Susan Christos, John Christos, Jackie Clinesmith, Silvia Coggin, William Steven Coggin, Shannon Conrad, Maria Contreras, Jean Cooper, Susan Cote, Mary M. Cotter, Anne Croteau, Bette Cundiff, Jennifer Curtsinger, Harold E. Davis, Suzette Davis, Art Denison, Antoinette Denison, Peggy Desportes, Wilma J. Devlin, Jackie Dombrowski, Joan Dotson, Yetta Dritch, Norman Dritch, Donald J. Driz, Mariline Dunn, Michael Ebert, Joanne Elam, John Elam, Irene Fauler, Suzanne R. Fausetin, Patty Findley, Kristine Fox, Jeanne Frazier, Audrey Ann Gambach, Andy Ganlen, Annette Geistfeld, Penny J. Goldwater, Linda Groves, Kara Grubis, Sheryl Harper, Michael Harpold, Virginia S. Harpold, Mary Hartsell, Kim C. Hatfield, Stephenie Herbranson, Rachel Herbranson, Rossana Hernandez, Janet R. Holt, Lisa R. Hyatt, Barbara J. James, Suzanne R. Johnson, David A. Johnson, Loree Johnson, Tom Johnson, Sandi Kilkuts, Beverly Kloehn, Heather Knee, Jack Knudson, Maureen Knudson, Mary Seu Larsen, Dick Larsen, Kathleen Lasky, George LeClair, Lila Lederman, Bernard Lederman, Carolyn Lerch, Gary Lerch, Susan Lichty, Paula Lipsitz, Pat Lizarraga, Cheri Lorochelle, Susan Luminoso, Zoralis Marquez, Ann W. Marsh, Gloria McInroy, Gretchen A.

McCabe, Sheri S. McManus, Pat Meurant, Audrey Mier, Caron Mitchell, Bessie C. Mooneyham, Grace Murphy, Larry Nagel, Ruth Neelans, Charlene Noland, Rachel O'Connor, Tamara Olson, Roger Olson, Mary Seu Peterka, Mary Pike, Mabel Polo, David Posqueiga, Pat Powers Williams, Tom Quick, Lyla L. Rath, Wendie Richardson, Melody Robinson, Lisa Robinson, Joan Robinson, Billie Rollins, Kevin Rotty, Mari Rotty, Krystal Rotty, Jorena Ruddy, Marilyn Runstadt, Sharon Rychener, Paul Saltzman, Jake Saltzman, Sarah Sammers, Gloria San Angelo, Peggy Sayre, Diane Scarpinato, Ann Scheib, Tracy Scholz, Jean Schroeter, Jane Schwartz, Kathleen Schwarz, Brenda Seeliger, Jill Shiba, Philip Silensky, Janet Sirbeck, Barbara B. Snyder, Jerry Snyder, Deb St. Alubin, Anna M. St. Louis, Jaxon Stallard, Nelle Starr, Jennifer Stephens, Annett Strack, Mike Strack, Robin Stroud, Nita Swift, Martha Swift, Eileen Thompson, Delene Toia, Nadine Torok, Richard Tuckett, M. J. Wieboldt, Shirley R. Wilbee, Sandy Wiley, Carol Wolf, Charles Wright, Jr., Joyce Yannuzzi and Beth Zucarelli.

DISCLAIMER

The recipes in this book have been our students' favorites and come from many sources. No recipe has been intentionally copied from another author.

We have a large support staff and student volunteers who work alongside the chef and the students to ensure everyone has fun in our kitchen.

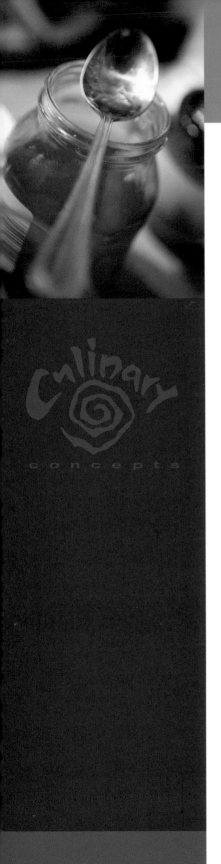

Culinary Concepts
AN EXTRAORDINARY COOKING SCHOOL

The Concept: Teaching people that cooking can be enjoyable, inspirational, economical, delicious and healthy. ✦ After teaching cooking for over 20 years and with both my children away at college, I decided to take the plunge and open my extraordinary cooking school in Tucson, Arizona. Extraordinary, because we focus on recipes and skills that are within the reach of every home cook. ✦ I had always taught demonstration classes but thought that a school that functioned along the lines of Guilliano Bugiali's school in Florence, Italy, was a better way to teach—an interactive school where students work alongside the instructor to create and become inspired.

In my classroom, we can have up to twenty-four students creating dishes at the same time. It is very organized chaos at times, but we get all the dishes finished and ready to serve at the same time. My teaching chefs have to know their recipes well, be able to see and direct in many different areas at the same time and know when dishes are or should be in the oven. They are the maestros of a culinary orchestra!

Our school has no particular style of cooking. Each teaching chef brings his or her own cooking style and specialty, so many of the recipes have international appeal. In every brochure we try to teach new classes with new recipes to keep the program updated and interesting.

I believe it is never too early to learn the cooking basics, so teaching children has always been an important part of our curriculum. Each year we include children's summer cooking camps, which are very popular. You can find a schedule of classes listed at www.culinaryconcepts.net.

Culinary Memories

My earliest cooking memories are of sitting in my high chair with my mother's personal cookbook. In New Zealand in those days, cookbooks were handwritten books of recipes handed down or passed along. My mother's book was an out-of-date diary that she would allow me to scribble in while she did her weekly baking

to fill the cookie tins. She would always cook a hot breakfast for us and, although she did not particularly enjoy cooking meals, she was an excellent baker. Cakes and cookies for morning and afternoon teas are an important part of life in New Zealand—even today.

When I went to school, baking production was stepped up as we all (my father and three younger sisters) took homemade lunches with us. Along with sandwiches (which I remember my mother making by the dozen every morning) and fruit, there were always two or three pieces of baked goodies in our lunch.

My grandparents had many fruit trees on their property and every summer the women of the family would spend days around the huge kitchen table, peeling, slicing and preparing fruit and vegetables to be preserved for the coming winter. Everyone had a storage room or closet put aside just for their jars and jams. Today, most of us who save food from one season to another use the freezer. The recipes in this book note if dishes can be frozen for use another day.

When I went to school, all girls were required to take home economics classes. In junior high, the home economic kitchen also had a small apartment-like kitchen and dining room attached where, in pairs, we were required twice a semester to spend the day cooking a three-course

lunch for a parent and our teacher. We were graded on how we prepared, served, conversed and cleaned up. I remember that I always asked my father to come to these lunches, though I do not remember what was served. I knew my father would enjoy eating anything I prepared.

I trained in New Zealand as a catering chef and then went back to Europe where I was fortunate enough to attend culinary schools in a number of different countries. My arrival in the United States was a compromise with my father, who continuously asked me to move closer to home. Los Angeles was halfway between Europe and New Zealand and I lived there three years before finally settling in Tucson.

When my children, Tim and Angela, were young, I found myself having to be our sole support. At this time I started "The Affair Catering" in Tucson, Arizona. Catering is very hard work, especially when you are the main planner, cook, server and clean-up person. With my sister-in-law and partner Jennie, plus a serving staff, we would cater up to four parties a night. No matter how tired I was, I always went home and cooked a meal for Tim and Angela for dinner the next evening if I was not going to be home. In fact, having dinner with them was such a priority that I would never do anything socially until after 7:00 p.m. so that I could cook and eat with them. Once a

month on a Saturday night we would have a family dinner party night. The children would choose the menu, help prepare the food, set the table, and we would dress and have a fun night dining in style.

When my daughter was a teenager I had a rude awakening when she informed me she was the only one in her class who was "forced" to sit down to dinner with her parents. Her friends ate when, where and how they wanted, usually fast food in front of the TV. I sincerely think that the fast-food culture, TV dinners, processed food packages and anything that is cooked in a microwave have undermined family dining. Not only is a civilized dining lifestyle compromised, but the basic physical and mental health of the individual and family are broken down. My goal at Culinary Concepts is to promote the joy and benefits of families and friends dining together.

Time to Learn to Cook

So often when it comes to mealtime, it is your brain that is bare, not the pantry. After cooking all day at Culinary Concepts, my drive home becomes a creative exercise. What do I have on hand that can be turned into dinner within the hour, without having to stop at the market?

I use the barbecue most nights. For me it is the easiest way to cook meat or fish. I buy my meat in quantity, vac-

uum seal it in single servings that I can bring out of the freezer and defrost it quickly in a bowl of cool water. (Defrosting meat in the microwave often partially cooks it, so I usually steer clear of that method.) By the time the barbecue is hot, the meat is defrosted. I have my salad made, vegetables in the steamer and my starch cooking. I use dry rubs or a splash of barbecue sauce on my meat, which cooks quickly on the barbecue or under the broiler.

When my children were at home I was much more organized. One day a week I would take the time to do menus for the following week plus make a shopping list. Grocery shopping was done once a week with a small pickup mid-week. I would also do a big cook once a week so dishes were ready in the freezer. This kept my food budget in line and the stress of evening meals to a minimum. If I was

running late, Tim and Angela knew what was planned and could start the dinner.

Presentation is everything. Don't put the saucepan on the table! I like to use big platters and serve the food family-style so people can help themselves. Serving buffet-style is another option, though I find with a family there is a lot of getting up and down from the table and often the first person through the buffet is finished and out the door before the last person sits down. When I was growing up, the food was portioned onto individual plates and brought to the table as they do in restaurants. Serve food whatever way works best for you, but do set a table and sit down together to eat. Even when eating alone I set the table as it is a great time to reflect on the day's events.

Each recipe in this book has tips on shortcuts, what can be made ahead, frozen and what to serve with the dish to make a complete meal. I find that to have an organized shopping list saves time, so make a list as you plan out your meals. And when you're done planning, take the time to enjoy cooking and spending time with your family.

Terminology Used In This Book

Baste: To moisten food as it cooks by brushing with butter, marinade, oil, pan juices or a sauce.

Blanch and parboil: To partially cook fruits and vegetables or to loosen the skins on almonds, peaches and tomatoes. Plunge into boiling water or place over steam. For vegetables, have a large bowl of iced water ready to chill them to preserve their color.

Blend: To combine several ingredients into a smooth mixture.

Boil: To heat a liquid until rolling bubbles, which cannot be stirred down, form.

Braise: To cook slowly on the stove or in the oven, in a covered pan with a small amount of liquid.

Brown: To cook food in a small amount of fat or oil in a hot pan over medium-high heat until the food becomes brown and the juices are sealed in.

Fold: A gentle blending action using a spatula when incorporating whipped cream or egg whites into another ingredient.

Julienne: To cut vegetables into long matchstick shapes about 2 inches long by 1/4 to 1/2 inch thick.

Marinate: To place food in a liquid mixture to tenderize and flavor.

Puree: To mash food into a smooth consistency.

Sauté: Sauté is a French word that translates into "fry." This method uses little butter and/or oil in a hot pan to cook the food until brown on the outside and cooked through.

Simmer: Liquids need to be brought up to a heat where there are small bubbles around the side of the pot. The simmer setting on your stove is usually too low to do this. Put the food over medium-high heat and bring to just under a boil, then turn the heat down to maintain the small bubbles around the side of the pot.

Steam: To cook food in a covered pan, on a rack or in a basket over boiling water.

Stir-fry: To quickly cook foods over high heat in a wok or pan, stirring constantly.

Zest: Finely grating the outside colored part of the skin of citrus fruit.

Alcohol Substitutes for Cooking Purposes

Amaretto (2 tablespoons): Substitute 1/2 teaspoon almond extract.

Brandy (equal amounts): Substitute white grape juice or apple cider.

Cointreau or Grand Marnier (1 tablespoon): Substitute 4 teaspoons orange juice, 1 teaspoon light Karo corn syrup, 1/2 teaspoon orange extract or 1 teaspoon orange zest or 1 1/2 teaspoons orange flower water.

Kahlua (1 tablespoon): Substitute 1/2 teaspoon instant coffee mixed with 2 tablespoons water.

Red wine (equal amounts): Substitute cranberry juice or red grape juice.

White wine (equal amounts): Substitute white grape juice or apple juice.

Maderia (1/4 cup): Substitute 1/4 cup Port, Sherry or red currant jelly.

Rum (1 tablespoon): Substitute 1 teaspoon rum extract mixed with 2 tablespoons apple juice.

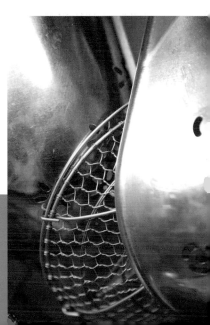

Our retail store features a beautiful selection of hand-painted Southwest pottery by local artists as well as imported pottery and fine French porcelain. We also stock a wide variety of regional sauces, oils and other seasonings along with "must have" cook's tools for the gourmet in all of us.

Appetizers

Appetizers are the small plates that are the first course to your dinner party. They usually take the place of a salad, or an appetizer can be a special plated salad. Remember not to fill your guests up before the main event. These small bites and little plates of food should tease the appetite. With cocktails before dinner, plan on three individual pieces of hors d'oeuvres per person and a dip or pâté that anyone really hungry can snack on. Heavy hors d'oeuvres usually means enough food so your guests do not need dinner. To me, this is the hardest entertaining. Making lots of hors d'oeuvres takes much more time than cooking a full meal. For this kind of a function, plan on some substantial finger foods like meat-filled bread rolls, large vegetable platters with dips and an assorted cheese tray. You can then fill in with about five pieces per person of your special small finger foods.

Belgian Endive with Smoked Salmon and Mustard Sauce

MUSTARD SAUCE
¼ cup Dijon mustard
2 tablespoons vegetable oil
1 teaspoon white wine vinegar

1 teaspoon brown sugar
1 teaspoon dried dill
½ pound thinly sliced smoked salmon
4 heads Belgian endive, separat-

ed, bottoms trimmed and rinsed
1 tablespoon drained capers
Parsley to garnish

MUSTARD SAUCE

1. Whisk all the ingredients together in a glass bowl and cover. This sauce will keep for up to a week.

2. To assemble, cut the salmon into small strips and twist up onto an endive leaf. Drizzle with the Mustard Sauce and sprinkle with a few capers. Arrange around the center of a decorative plate and place parsley in the center.

[MAKES ABOUT 24 PIECES]

Avocados with Shrimp Salad

TOPPING
¾ cup mayonnaise
1 green onion, chopped
1 very small clove garlic, crushed
1 small tomato, peeled, seeded

and chopped
1 teaspoon capers, chopped
¼ cup chopped green bell pepper
½ jalapeno, seeded and chopped (or more to taste)
Salt and pepper

1 teaspoon chopped cilantro

6 whole leaves butter lettuce
3 ripe avocados
12 cooked medium shrimp
Cilantro leaves for garnish

1. In a glass bowl, gently fold all the topping ingredients together and then set aside.

2. Wash the lettuce leaves and gently spin to get rid of the moisture. Place one on each of six plates.

3. Cut the avocados in half and remove the pit by hitting and twisting it with a sharp knife. Fill the avocado pit hole with the topping or, with a spoon, remove the avocado fruit from the skin and slice into thin slices. Place in the lettuce leaf. Top with the topping mixture and garnish with a whole shrimp and a whole cilantro leaf.

[SERVES 6 TO 8]

Serve two Salmon Cakes on a lettuce leaf with the Citrus Tartar Sauce as a first course.

Salmon Cakes with Citrus Tartar Sauce

1½ pounds salmon, minced
2 teaspoons grated lemon zest
4 teaspoons lemon juice
3 teaspoons soy sauce
¼ cup mayonnaise
2 teaspoons minced jalapeno
2 tablespoons minced fresh ginger
1 teaspoon dried dill
2 tablespoons dried breadcrumbs

2 tablespoons beaten egg (use the rest of the egg in an omelet)
1 cup panko (Japanese bread-crumbs)
Vegetable oil
Lettuce leaves

CITRUS TARTAR SAUCE
½ cup mayonnaise
1 tablespoon lime juice

½ teaspoon Worcestershire sauce
½ teaspoon Tabasco
Salt to taste
½ teaspoon orange zest
½ teaspoon orange juice
½ teaspoon sugar
1 tablespoon grated fresh ginger
1 tablespoon chopped cilantro

1. In a medium bowl, mix together the salmon, lemon zest and juice, soy sauce, mayonnaise, jalapeno, ginger, dill, bread-crumbs and egg. Using a small ice cream scoop for uniformity, form salmon mixture into small 2-inch patties and roll in the panko.
2. Heat about 2 tablespoons vegetable oil in a medium frying pan and sauté the salmon cakes until golden brown on each side. Serve the Salmon Cakes on lettuce leaves with the Citrus Tartar Sauce.

CITRUS TARTAR SAUCE
3. Mix all ingredients together. This sauce will keep in the refrigerator for up to one week.

[MAKES 24 DOLLAR-SIZED SALMON CAKES]

These have been a staff favorite. They are easy to make and can be frozen before cooking.

Sausage Rolls

2 tablespoons butter
1 medium onion, finely chopped
1½ pounds ground pork butt or turkey
1 teaspoon herbes de Provence

4 drops Tabasco
1 teaspoon Worcestershire sauce
1 teaspoon salt
few grinds fresh pepper
1 egg, beaten

1 package frozen puff pastry, thawed in the refrigerator
1 egg yolk
1 tablespoon water

1. In a medium frying pan, melt the butter and add the onion. Sauté until the onion is soft, about 10 minutes. Remove from the pan and place onto a plate to cool. In a bowl, mix together the meat, herbs and seasonings. When the onion has cooled, mix into the meat with the beaten egg. Place into a piping bag without a tip.

2. Preheat the oven to 450 degrees F.

3. Separate the two sheets of pastry and roll one into about a 10 x 14-inch rectangle. Cut into 4 strips lengthwise, each about 2 1/2 inches wide. Pipe a line using half of the sausage mixture along the strip of pastry about 1 inch from the edge. Repeat with the second pastry.

4. In a small bowl mix the egg yolk with the water to make an egg wash. Brush the edge of the pastry with the egg wash and fold the pastry over to enclose the meat. With a fork, press the two edges of the pastry together to seal. At 1 1/2-inch intervals, cut through the long roll to make individual sausage rolls. Make two small slits in the top of each sausage roll and then brush the outside of the roll with the egg wash.

5. Place on a baking sheet lined with parchment paper or a silicone mat, leaving about a 3/4-inch space between each roll. Cook at 450 degrees F for 10 minutes, reduce the heat to 350 degrees F and cook them 10 minutes more, or until the pastry is nicely browned.

HINT: The rolls can be frozen before they are cooked. Do not defrost them before cooking; instead bake them at 450 degrees F for 10 minutes and lower the heat to 350 degrees F and bake for 20 minutes more.

[MAKES ABOUT 50 SAUSAGE ROLLS]

Serve this cheesecake with cocktails or as part of a buffet table.

Gazpacho Cheesecake

CRUST
1 cup crushed Wheat Thins
3 tablespoons butter, melted

FILLING
2 Roma tomatoes
1 red bell pepper

1 tablespoon gelatin
¼ cup water
12 ounces cream cheese, at room
   temperature
2 cups tomato juice
⅛ teaspoon Tabasco
½ teaspoon chili powder

1 stalk celery, finely chopped
2 green onions, finely chopped
2 tablespoons chopped parsley
1 European cucumber, thinly
   sliced for garnish
6 shrimp to garnish (optional)

1. To make the crust, put the crushed crackers into a food processor and then add the melted butter; gently blend together. Press into the bottom of an 8-inch springform pan. Place in the refrigerator to set.

2. Preheat the broiler and a small saucepan of water.

3. Skin the tomatoes by cutting an X in the top and dropping them into boiling water for 30 seconds. Cool, peel the skin off, scoop out the seeds and finely chop the flesh.

4. Cut the red pepper in half, cut out the ribs and the seeds. Place on a baking sheet and flatten with your hand. Place under the broiler until the skin has blistered. Put into a plastic or paper bag to sweat for 10 minutes, then peel and chop.

5. Sprinkle the gelatin over the water, allow to soften for a couple of minutes and then gently heat in the microwave until it is dissolved and clear. In a separate bowl, using an electric mixer, beat the cream cheese and slowly add the tomato juice, Tabasco, chili powder and gelatin mixture.

6. Allow the filling to cool either in the refrigerator or set the bowl of filling over a bowl of ice, until it has almost set. Fold in the chopped tomato, red pepper, celery, green onion and parsley. Pour onto the base and chill for several hours or overnight. Unmold and decorate with the thinly sliced cucumber and optional shrimp. Cut into thin slices and serve with French bread or Melba toast.

[MAKES 16 WEDGE SERVINGS]

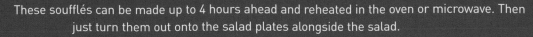
These soufflés can be made up to 4 hours ahead and reheated in the oven or microwave. Then just turn them out onto the salad plates alongside the salad.

Hot Goat Cheese Soufflé with Arugula Salad

2 tablespoons softened butter to grease dishes
2 tablespoons unsalted butter
2 tablespoons all-purpose flour
1 cup hot milk
4 ounces goat cheese
¼ cup grated Romano cheese
1 teaspoon dry mustard
2 drops Tabasco
2 eggs, separated
¼ teaspoon salt
¼ teaspoon white pepper
⅛ teaspoon fresh nutmeg

SALAD
¼ cup hazelnuts
½ teaspoon Dijon mustard
pinch salt and pepper
2 tablespoons white wine vinegar
2 tablespoons hazelnut oil
2 tablespoons olive oil
8 cups arugula or baby spinach
Romano cheese ribbons (use a potato peeler)

1. Preheat the oven to 375 degrees F. Brush the insides of six 4-ounce ramekins with the softened butter.

2. In a medium saucepan, over medium heat, melt the butter, add the flour and cook for 1 minute. Stir in the hot milk and cook until the mixture has thickened. Add the goat cheese, Romano cheese, mustard and Tabasco. Stir over low heat until the cheeses have melted. Pour into a medium-large bowl. Whisk in the egg yolks one at a time, followed by the salt, pepper and nutmeg.

3. Using an electric beater, beat the egg whites until stiff. Gently fold the egg whites into the egg yolk mixture. Spoon into the ramekins.

4. Prepare a water bath for cooking. Heat about 6 cups of water to boiling point. Line the bottom of a roasting dish or pan with at least 1-inch sides and that is large enough to hold six ramekins with four layers of paper towels. Place the soufflé dishes in the pan and then once in the oven, pour enough hot water onto the paper towels to come halfway up the sides of the ramekins. Cook until the soufflés are puffed and lightly browned, about 20 minutes. Carefully remove from the water bath. The soufflés will hold at this point for several hours and can be served hot or at room temperature. Run a knife around the inside of the ramekin and invert onto a plate.

5. For the salad, put the hazelnuts onto a baking sheet and place in the oven. They can go into the oven above the soufflés. Cook the hazelnuts until the skins have turned a deep brown and the nut meat is lightly browned. Pour the nuts onto the top half of a dry kitchen towel, cover the nuts with the bottom half of the towel and rub them well to loosen the skins. Not all the skin will come off. Roughly chop the nuts.

6. Whisk together the Dijon mustard, salt, pepper and vinegar. Slowly whisk in the oils. Pour as much of the dressing as needed over the greens, serve to one side of the goat cheese soufflé and garnish with the Romano cheese ribbons and chopped hazelnuts.

[SERVES 6]

You can make this a quick hors d'oeuvre by buying the pizza dough and the pesto already prepared.

Mini Pesto Pizzas with Shrimp and Artichokes

PIZZA DOUGH

1 package dry yeast
1 teaspoon sugar
¼ cup slightly warm water (no more than 100 degrees F)
¼ cup slightly warm milk (no more than 100 degrees F)
2 tablespoons olive oil
1 teaspoon salt
½ cup whole wheat flour

½ cup all-purpose flour, plus more for kneading, if needed
2 tablespoons cornmeal

PESTO SAUCE

2 tablespoons pine nuts, toasted
1 cup basil leaves, firmly packed
1 clove garlic, crushed
2 tablespoons grated Parmesan cheese

⅓ cup extra virgin olive oil

TOPPING

12 bottled artichoke hearts (not marinated), cut in half
24 large shrimp, shelled, cooked and cut in half lengthwise
1 cup grated mozzarella cheese
½ cup Romano cheese

PIZZA DOUGH

1. Place the yeast and sugar in a medium bowl. Add the water, milk and olive oil; stir to blend. Allow to sit until you can see the yeast begin to bubble, about 10 minutes. Stir in the salt, whole wheat flour and as much of the all-purpose flour as needed to make the dough firm enough to handle. Turn the dough out onto a floured surface and knead until smooth, adding more flour if needed. The dough should be soft and pliable. Place the dough in a large oiled bowl, cover and allow to rise in a warm place until doubled in size, about 1 hour. Turn out onto a floured board and cut into 24 uniform pieces. Roll each piece into a 2-inch round and put onto a corn-meal dusted baking sheet.

PESTO

2. Puree the pine nuts, basil, garlic and cheese in a blender or food processor. Slowly add the olive oil. This pesto can be made ahead and frozen for up to 3 months.

3. Preheat the oven to 450 degrees F.

4. Spread the pizza dough with the Pesto, top with a piece of artichoke heart, 2 shrimp halves and some mozzarella and Romano cheeses. Bake for 10 minutes, or until the pizzas are lightly browned.

HINT: Use only the leaves of fresh herbs. The stems are woody and only add fiber to dishes.

HINT: When adding liquid to yeast, it needs to be only warm, no more than 100 degrees F. Over 100 degrees F and you will kill the yeast.

HINT: To toast pine nuts put them into a dry frying pan and cook them over medium-low heat, stirring occasionally, until they are browned. Watch carefully because they burn easily.

[MAKES 24 MINI PIZZAS]

Setting Up Class

1

1. Instructing staff on how we are going to set up the recipes and ingredients before class begins.

2. The school set up with chairs, aprons and recipes in place, ready for the students.

3. Special recipe books prepared for the debutantes attending a class as part of their pre-Cotillion festivities.

4. Two of the debs with their "cooking" T-shirts.

A pikelet is an English word for something that looks like a dollar pancake. If you cannot find Mexican chorizo, you can substitute spicy Italian sausage.

Potato and Chorizo Pikelets with Guacamole

2   medium white potatoes
½   teaspoon salt
1   cup Mexican chorizo
1   cup plain yogurt
1   cup milk
2   eggs, well whisked

½   teaspoon chopped chipotle
    chile in adobo sauce
1   clove garlic, minced
2   tablespoons chopped cilantro
¼   cup chopped green onions
1   cup flour

1   teaspoon baking powder
½   teaspoon salt
Freshly ground pepper
Vegetable oil for cooking
Guacamole (page 59)
Cilantro

1. Peel the potatoes and cut in half. Put into a pot with the salt and just cover with cold water. Bring to a boil and cook until still slightly crunchy. Drain and cool until you can handle them and grate on the largest grater setting.
2. In a small frying pan, cook the chorizo until lightly browned, drain on a paper towel.
3. In a medium bowl, whisk together the yogurt, milk and eggs. Stir in the chipotle chile, garlic, cilantro, green onions, chorizo and potato. In another bowl, sift together the flour, baking powder, salt and pepper. Stir into the potato mixture.
4. Brush a thin layer of oil onto the bottom of a large frying pan. Heat over medium-high heat until the oil is hot but not smoking. Using a teaspoon, carefully drop small spoonfuls of the potato mixture into the pan and cook until browned on both sides, turning only once. Put onto a serving platter and once cooled top with a small spoon full of guacamole and garnish with a cilantro leaf.

[MAKES 24 PIKELETS]

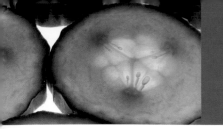

Everyone enjoys a plate of raw vegetables with a flavorful dip.
For a variation in display, stand celery sticks, including some with leaves,
and Belgian endive in decorative wine/tall glasses.

Cucumber-Shrimp Dip

½ cucumber
1 teaspoon salt
6 ounces cream cheese, at room temperature
½ cup sour cream
1 teaspoon lemon juice

12 medium shrimp, cooked and minced
2 eggs, hard-boiled and finely chopped
¼ cup finely chopped celery
1 tablespoon chopped fresh parsley

1 tablespoon chopped fresh chives
1 tablespoon chopped fresh tarragon
½ clove garlic, crushed
1 small shallot, minced
¼ teaspoon salt
Pinch white pepper
3 drops Tabasco

1. Peel, seed and grate the cucumber. Place into a strainer over a bowl and sprinkle with the salt. Let it drain for 15 minutes, rinse with cold water and squeeze dry.

2. With an electric mixer or in a food processor, mix the cream cheese, sour cream and lemon juice until smooth. Transfer to a non-metallic bowl. Stir in the cucumber, shrimp, eggs, celery, herbs, garlic, shallot, salt, pepper and Tabasco.

3. Serve with fresh vegetables of your choice. This dip is best used within 2 days. It is also a great filling for avocados.

[MAKES 2 1/2 CUPS]

Chile-Cheese Straws

1½ cups plus 2 tablespoons all-purpose flour
1 teaspoon baking powder

½ teaspoon salt
1½ teaspoons red chile powder
6 tablespoons butter, chilled

2 cups grated extra-sharp cheddar cheese
4 tablespoons cold water

1. Preheat the oven to 425 degrees F. Sift the flour, baking powder, salt and chile powder into a medium bowl. Cut the chilled butter into small pieces and rub into the flour with your fingers or with a pastry blender. The butter mixture should resemble small grains of rice. Mix in the cheese and then sprinkle over the water using a spoon or your hand to form it into a ball. Do not over-work.

2. On a floured board, quickly roll the dough out into a rectangle about 3/8 inch thick. Cut into straws about 1/2 inch wide and 4 inches long.

3. Bake on a parchment paper-lined baking sheet for 10 to 15 minutes, or until crisp and lightly browned.

[MAKES ABOUT 24 CHEESE STRAWS]

This mousse has been one of my favorites to serve as an hors d'oeuvre. Easy to make and best if made two or three days before you serve it.

Chicken Liver Mousse

2 tablespoons butter	½ cup butter	¼ cup whipping cream
2 medium shallots, finely chopped	1 teaspoon salt	
	⅛ teaspoon allspice	ASPIC:
½ pound chicken livers	⅛ teaspoon pepper	¼ teaspoon gelatin
⅓ cup Madeira wine	⅛ teaspoon dried thyme	¼ cup Chicken Stock (page 72) or water

1. Over medium heat, melt the butter in a medium frying pan. Add the shallots and sauté for about 2 minutes, or until they soften. Add the chicken livers and cook gently, being careful not to overcook—they should still be a little pink inside. Pour the livers and the shallots into the bowl of a food processor.

2. Add the wine to the same pan and cook until reduced by half. Pour into the food processor bowl with the livers. Cut the butter into pieces and melt in the same frying pan. Add to the food processor along with the sea-sonings and the whipping cream. Process until smooth. Strain the mixture through a sieve to remove the solids into a 1 1/2 cup serving bowl; chill well. Decorate the top with a green onion stem and a carrot flower. Cover in Aspic.

3. To make the Aspic, dissolve the gelatin in the liquid for about 2 minutes. Heat gently in the microwave to dissolve. Allow to cool and then pour over the top of the mousse.

4. Serve with thinly sliced French bread, Melba toast or water crackers.

[SERVES 8 TO 10 FOR COCKTAILS]

You can make this in one mold and serve as part of a buffet table or you can make them as pictured in small molds and serve them as appetizers. If you do not have the small fish molds, they also work well turned out of a small ramekin.

Salmon Mousse

1   tablespoon butter
½   pound salmon
1½ teaspoons gelatin
2   tablespoons red wine vinegar
2   ounces cream cheese

1   small clove garlic
4   tablespoons mayonnaise
2   drops Tabasco
¼   teaspoon lemon juice
¼   teaspoon salt

pinch white pepper
½   pound Roma tomatoes (about 3
    medium), peeled and seeded
    (page 142)

1. In a small frying pan, melt the butter and sauté the salmon gently until cooked through. Flake and discard any bones. Put into a food processor. Soften the gelatin in the red wine vinegar, heat gently to dissolve and then add to the salmon. Add the remaining ingredients and puree in the processor until smooth. Pour into 10 individual molds or one 2-cup mold. Allow to set in the refrigerator. Use within two days as the fish begins to taste stronger.

[SERVES 10]

Roquefort Dip

4   ounces cream cheese, at room
    temperature
3   tablespoons milk
2   teaspoons dry sherry

4   ounces Roquefort cheese
2   heads Belgian endive, either
    green or purple
2   Granny Smith apples

2   pears
1   lemon
wooden cocktail skewers

1. With an electric mixer, blend together the cream cheese, milk and sherry. Stir in the Roquefort cheese, leaving some lumps.
2. Cut the ends of the Belgian endive, separate and wash the spears. Lay them out on a platter.

3. Cut the apples and pears into quarters and remove the cores. Cut each quarter in half, put in a bowl and sprinkle with lemon juice. Spear each piece of fruit with a skewer and arrange on the endive leaves. This dip will keep for up to a week.

[SERVES 8]

Serve this dip with Belgian endive spears, and apple and pear skewers.

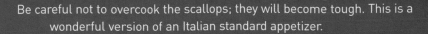
Be careful not to overcook the scallops; they will become tough. This is a wonderful version of an Italian standard appetizer.

Scallops Provençal Bruschetta

1 loaf French bread cut into diagonal slices ½ inch thick
Olive oil
¼ cup all-purpose flour
½ teaspoon salt
Few grinds pepper
½ pound bay scallops
4 tablespoons olive oil, use more if needed

2 tablespoons finely chopped onion
¼ pound mushrooms, sliced
4 cloves garlic, minced
2 Roma tomatoes, skinned, seeded and chopped
½ teaspoon tomato paste
2 teaspoons pitted and chopped kalamata olives

¼ cup chopped roasted red pepper (can use ready prepared)
2 tablespoons red wine or 2 teaspoons red wine vinegar
½ teaspoon salt
4 grinds pepper
3 tablespoons thinly sliced fresh basil

1. Preheat the broiler.
2. Brush each side of the bread with olive oil and lightly brown each side under the broiler. Arrange on a serving platter.
3. Stir the flour, salt and pepper together. Pat the scallops dry and then toss in the seasoned flour.
4. In a frying pan over medium-high heat, heat the 4 tablespoons of olive oil. Separate the scallops and sauté in the oil until lightly browned, about 1 minute on each side. Brown but do not overcook. Take out of the pan and set aside on a plate. Add the onion, mushrooms and garlic to the pan and cook for about 3 minutes, or until the mushroom juices have evaporated. Add the tomatoes, tomato paste, olives, red peppers and red wine. Mix lightly together and season with salt and pepper. Cook until well blended and heated through. Add the scallops and stir together.
5. Take off the heat. Taste to make sure you have enough salt; stir in the basil. Spoon a spoonful onto each bruschetta. Serve hot or at room temperature.

HINT: This topping is also good tossed served over hot pasta and sprinkled with a little grated Parmesan cheese.

[MAKES 30 SERVINGS]

This simple-to-put-together dish makes a delicious first course. Serve three ravioli per person.

Spinach Ravioli with Chile-Tomato Cream Sauce

SAUCE
- 2 tablespoons olive oil
- 2 tablespoons finely chopped white onion
- 2 cloves garlic, chopped
- 1 (28-ounce) can peeled Italian tomatoes, good quality

Salt and pepper to taste
- 1 small chipotle chile in adobo sauce, finely chopped
- ¼ cup water, if needed
- ½ cup heavy cream

Cilantro sprigs
- ¼ cup pine nuts, toasted and chopped

RAVIOLI
- 7 ounces frozen spinach, thawed
- 1 egg
- 8 ounces ricotta cheese
- ½ teaspoon salt
- ⅛ teaspoon pepper
- 1 package wonton wrappers

SAUCE

1. Pour the olive oil into a medium skillet over medium heat. Add the onion, cover and wilt for about 3 minutes. Take off the cover, add the garlic and sauté for 1 minute. Add the tomatoes (crush them in your hand) and liquid, salt, pepper and chipotle chile. Reduce the heat to low so the sauce just simmers and simmer for 30 minutes. If the sauce gets too thick, add the 1/4 cup water.

2. Put the sauce into a food processor or blender to puree and strain through a fairly coarse strainer. Return to a medium heat. Heat the cream to a similar temperature as the sauce and combine the two. Do not bring to a boil.

RAVIOLI

3. Line a baking sheet with parchment paper and set aside. Squeeze all the moisture out of the spinach and chop finely. In a medium mixing bowl, mix together the spinach, egg, ricotta cheese, salt and pepper.

4. Place three or four wonton wrappers on a work surface. Spoon a teaspoon of the filling into the middle of each wonton. Do not overfill or they will burst while cooking. Brush around the edges of the wonton with a little water, fold to form a triangle, then press the seams to seal and place on the parchment paper. Repeat until all the wrappers and filling are used.

5. Bring a large pot of water to boil. Once the water is boiling, add some salt and carefully lower the ravioli into the boiling water, about 6 at a time. As soon as they float to the top they are cooked. With a slotted spoon remove them from the water and arrange on a plate.

6. To serve, place three or four ravioli on a plate and spoon a little sauce over top. Garnish with a sprig of cilantro and a sprinkling of pine nuts.

[MAKES 40 RAVIOLI]

Working with Filo (Phyllo) Dough

People seem to be so intimidated by this thin flour and water dough, however, it is really easy to work with once you understand how to deal with it.

I have only once made filo by hand. Rita Rosenberg, a dear friend and fellow culinary instructor, grew up in Munich where she would make and stretch the dough by hand for her wonderful strudels. Truthfully, although the flavor and texture were really good, that was far too much work.

There are many brands of filo to be found in the frozen food section of your market. In my recipes I refer to a sheet as one that is 9 x 14 inches rather than the half sheets that I have seen being sold recently. If you happen to buy the smaller sheets, use two sheets instead of folding one sheet in half.

Defrosting Filo

Filo is mostly bought frozen. It has to be defrosted slowly so that it does not become sticky and gum together. Do not defrost in the microwave—trust me, I have tried it! Allow your filo to defrost overnight in its package in the refrigerator. Bring it to room temperature about 1 hour before you unwrap it.

Using Filo

Have your filling, melted butter and a soft pastry brush ready before the filo is unwrapped. Once unwrapped, place it on a sheet of parchment or wax paper, completely cover it with another sheet of paper and then top with a well rung out damp towel. You need to be quick once you take a sheet of filo out from under the towel and paper—if the filo dries out before it is buttered, it will become dry and brittle and

almost impossible to use. Gently lift off one sheet of filo and place on a work surface. Replace the paper-towel topping. Quickly and lightly brush the entire sheet of filo with butter, right to the edges. Repeat as per the instructions in the recipe you are doing.

If a sheet of filo should tear or stick to the next one, you can stick the pieces together with a brush of butter. Make filo work for you, do not become frustrated with it. It flakes and breaks everywhere once it is cooked anyway.

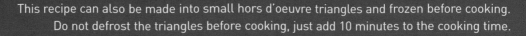
This recipe can also be made into small hors d'oeuvre triangles and frozen before cooking. Do not defrost the triangles before cooking, just add 10 minutes to the cooking time.

Judith's Spinakopita

½ cup butter
1½ cups chopped onions
½ pound mushrooms, thinly
   sliced

2 pounds frozen spinach, thawed
   (preferably whole leaf)
5 eggs
1 teaspoon dried dill
1 teaspoon salt

4 grinds fresh pepper
¾ pounds feta cheese, crumbled
½ cup chopped green onions
1 package filo dough, thawed
½ cup butter, melted

1. In a large frying pan, melt the butter. Add the onions and sauté over medium heat until soft and tender, about 5 minutes. Add the mushrooms and cook until their juices evaporate. Remove from the heat and pour into a large bowl to cool.

2. Squeeze the spinach in a clean towel until very dry. Chop with a knife or in a food processor and then add to the cooled onion mixture.

3. In another bowl, whisk the eggs with the dill, salt and pepper. Fold into the spinach mixture along with the feta and green onions.

4. Preheat the oven to 375 degrees F.

5. Unfold the filo and cover with parchment paper and a damp towel. Butter a 9 x 13-inch

baking dish. Using one sheet at a time, gently but quickly brush each layer with melted butter, repeating with 10 sheets of filo, buttering the top of each sheet well before adding the next. Spread the filling over the top of the 10 filo sheets and top with the remaining filo, buttering each layer between the sheets.

6. Refrigerate for 10 minutes to allow the butter to set. With a sharp knife, cut the top layers of filo into squares. Bake for 30 minutes, or until the filo is golden brown. Cool for 10 minutes and then cut all the way through into serving pieces.

HINT: In a class taught a while back, we added one pound of cooked ground lamb to the filling, cooked it in a 9 x 13-inch pan and served it cut into squares for lunch, with a salad. The ground lamb was a great addition.

[MAKES 15 PIECES, 2½ X 2 INCHES EACH]

Any of these filo fillings can also be used to fill store-bought puff pastry.

Filo Triangles with Wild Mushroom Filling

6 tablespoons olive oil	1 cup chopped green onions	1 teaspoon salt
2 tablespoons chopped shallots	2 pounds wild mushrooms,	½ teaspoon freshly ground pepper
1 tablespoon minced garlic	sliced (mixture of any fresh	1 egg, beaten with a whisk
1 tablespoon chopped fresh	mushrooms)	½ package filo (about 10 sheets),
thyme or 1 teaspoon dried	½ cup dry white wine	at room temperature
thyme	1 teaspoon paprika	1 cup unsalted butter, melted
	1 cup grated Parmesan cheese	

1. In a large sauté pan, over medium-low heat, heat the olive oil. Add the shallots, garlic, thyme and green onions. Cook until wilted, about 5 minutes. Turn up the heat to medium-high and add the mushrooms; sauté for about 10 minutes, or until their juices have evaporated. Add the wine and paprika, and then cook until the wine has evaporated. Transfer to a large bowl and cool for about 5 minutes. Add the cheese, salt, pepper and egg; blend together.

2. Preheat the oven to 400 degrees F.

3. Open the filo and cover with parchment paper and a damp towel. Peel off one sheet and gently but quickly brush it with melted butter. Top it with a second sheet of filo and brush that sheet with butter. Cut the filo sheets into 2-inch-wide strips and put 1 teaspoon of filling in the middle of each; roll up into a triangle and brush with more melted butter. Cook for 5 to 10 minutes, or until they are golden brown.

HINT: For store-bought puff pastry, roll the pastry out a little thinner and cut into 3-inch rounds. Mix an egg yolk with 1 tablespoon of water and use to moisten the edges. Fill the center with 1 teaspoon of filling, fold over into a half-moon and seal the edges with a fork. Brush the entire pastry with the egg wash and cook as you would the filo.

HINT: Filo triangles can be frozen before they are cooked. Take them straight from the freezer to the oven and defrost/cook for about 20 minutes. Do not defrost them before you put them in the oven.

[MAKES 48 TRIANGLES]

There are many fillings you can use to fill these hors d'oeuvres!
Roll them up as shown in the photo.

Filo Triangles

SPICY LAMB FILLING
1 pound ground lamb
1 medium yellow onion, chopped
1 large clove garlic, minced
½ teaspoon salt

1 teaspoon cinnamon
½ teaspoon allspice
2 tablespoons currants
4 grinds pepper
2 tablespoons chopped parsley

2 ounces goat cheese
½ pound filo (about 10 sheets), defrosted
¾ cup butter, melted

1. Heat a medium frying pan and add the lamb. When it has browned, add the onion and cook until the onion is soft; drain off any excess fat. Add the garlic, salt, cinnamon, allspice, currants, pepper and parsley. Cook for 2 minutes, and then cool. Stir in the goat cheese.

2. Preheat to oven to 400 degrees F.

3. Unfold the filo and cover with parchment paper and a damp towel. Place one sheet on the workspace and gently brush all over with melted butter. Top with a second sheet and butter well. Cut into 2-inch-wide strips. Place a teaspoonful of the filling in the lower corner of the strip. Start folding in triangles until you reach the top of the strip. Butter the triangle well and place on a cookie sheet; repeat. Bake for 15 minutes, or until the filo is golden brown.

[MAKES 30 TRIANGLES]

This is a delicious luncheon or vegetable dish, or a vegetarian alternative.

Vegetable Strudel

1 onion
3 cloves garlic, crushed
2 tablespoons butter
2 tablespoons vegetable oil
1 eggplant, peeled and cut into ½-inch dice
¾ pound zucchini, cut into ½-inch dice
1 red pepper, cut into ½-inch dice
½ pound mushrooms, diced

2 tablespoons tomato paste
2 tablespoons chopped parsley
¼ teaspoon dried thyme
1 teaspoon salt
¼ teaspoon pepper
10 sheets filo pastry
⅓ cup vegetable oil
2 tablespoons grated Parmesan cheese

CHEESE SAUCE
2 tablespoons butter
2 tablespoons flour
1 cup hot milk, heated in the microwave
2 tablespoons grated Parmesan cheese
¼ cup grated sharp cheddar cheese
2 drops Tabasco
Salt and white pepper to taste

1. Finely chop the onion and garlic. Heat the butter and oil in a large pan until hot. Add the onion and cook for 5 minutes. Stir in the garlic and cook another 2 minutes. Add the eggplant, zucchini, red pepper and mushrooms. Cook for 2 minutes, stirring occasionally. Stir in the tomato paste, parsley, thyme, salt and pepper. Pour the mixture into a bowl to cool slightly.

2. Preheat the oven to 375 degrees F.

3. Working on a piece of parchment paper or a silicone mat, layer the filo dough, brushing each sheet lightly with oil until you have layered all 10 sheets. Spoon the vegetable mixture along the long side of the filo and, using the parchment to help you roll, roll the filo around the vegetable mixture. Using the parchment, lift the strudel onto a baking sheet, leaving the parchment underneath it. Brush the top of the strudel with oil and sprinkle with the Parmesan cheese. Score through the top few layers of filo on the diagonal to make 8 slices (do not cut all the way through to the vegetables; this scoring is just to help with slicing to serve). Cook for about 30 minutes, or until golden brown. Serve with Cheese Sauce.

CHEESE SAUCE

4. Melt the butter in a small saucepan and add the flour. Cook for 1 minute, and then stir in the hot milk and bring to a boil. Add the cheeses, Tabasco, and salt and pepper. Take off the heat and keep warm, or cool and reheat before using. If the sauce gets too thick, thin with a little more milk.

[SERVES 8]

This can be used as a dip and a topping for the Potato and Chorizo Pikelets.

Guacamole

2 large or 3 small ripe avocados
3 tablespoons lime juice
1 medium tomato, chopped

½ cup finely chopped green onion
2 jalapenos, finely chopped (see hint)

1 small clove garlic, minced
½ teaspoon salt and a few twists of pepper
2 teaspoons chopped cilantro

1. Cut the avocado in half around the pit. Twist to separate the halves. Hit the pit with the sharp blade of your knife, and then twist to release the pit. With a spoon, scoop out the avocado flesh. Mash with a fork or potato masher, leaving lumps for texture. Fold in the remaining ingredients and stir gently to blend. Use the guacamole soon after you make it.

HINT: See page 142 for information on cutting a jalapeno.

[MAKES 2 CUPS]

Artichokes Stuffed with Seafood

4 large artichokes
½ lemon
2 teaspoons salt

FILLING
2 tablespoons butter

½ pound medium shrimp, shelled and deveined
½ pound bay scallops
½ pound crabmeat
1 cup mayonnaise
2 tablespoons lemon juice
1 teaspoon prepared horseradish

1 tablespoon red seafood sauce or ketchup
¼ teaspoon Worcestershire sauce
3 drops Tabasco
2 tablespoons chopped parsley
Parsley sprigs

1. With a pair of scissors, cut the sharp tips off all the artichoke leaves. Slice off the top inch of the artichoke and slice the stem ends close, so they will sit on plates. Squeeze the lemon into enough cold water to cover the artichokes and put the trimmed artichokes into the water to stop them going brown.

2. Bring to a boil a pot of water large enough to immerse the whole artichokes. Add the salt and the trimmed artichokes. Do not discard the lemon water. Weight the artichokes down so they stay submerged with a saucepan lid. Cook until an artichoke leaf will easily pull off, about 20 minutes. Have about 6 cups of ice ready in a large bowl and add the reserved lemon water. As soon as the artichokes are cooked, use a slotted spoon to take them out of the boiling water and put into the iced lemon water to chill.

3. When the artichokes have cooled down, take them out of the water. With your fingers, pull out the very center leaves so you expose the furry "choke." With a small spoon scoop out the fuzzy choke, being careful to leave the tender bottom intact. Turn upside down onto a paper towel to drain. The artichokes will last 2 days in the refrig-

erator once drained. Turn them up on their stems so the leaves do not get bruised.

4. To make the filling, melt the butter in a small pan and gently cook the shrimp just until they turn pink. Remove the shrimp from the pan to cool (you can also use ready-cooked shrimp). Add the bay scallops and sauté gently for about 3 minutes. Remove the scallops from the pan and cool.

5. Put aside 4 shrimp for the garnish and chop the remainder into about 6 pieces each. In a glass or nonreactive bowl, combine all of the seafood. In another bowl, mix together the mayonnaise, lemon juice, horseradish, seafood sauce, Worcestershire sauce, Tabasco and parsley. Gently fold the mayonnaise mixture into the seafood. Taste for salt and pepper. Allow to sit for about 1 hour before filling the artichokes. Fill the center of the artichoke with the seafood mixture. Garnish with one of the reserved whole shrimp and a sprig of parsley.

6. To eat, pull off a leaf and scoop a little filling onto it. You only eat the top meaty part of the end of the leaf and make a pile of leaves before you get to the artichoke heart. This is your prize and you can savor eating the tender artichoke heart.

[SERVES 4]

Soups

Soup is the ultimate comfort food. Soups are easy to make and many freeze well. They can be a complete meal, a cool, light first course or a luncheon dish. 🐟 At Culinary Concepts the first class we have in the certificate course is on how to make your own basic stock. In the school we make all our stocks and freeze them in 1-cup and 4-cup increments. You do not need to make your own stock to make good soup. There are good tasting stocks in the markets that you can buy; however, they usually have a high sodium content. So if you use store-bought stock, be careful about the amount of salt you use in these recipes. 🐟 Making your own stock can be very satisfying.

Ahh, the miraculous, never-ending varieties of soup. It can be simple, complicated, rich, or light,
delighting the vegetarian, gourmet dieter, and, of course, those of us who just
plain love to dream up new dishes straight from the pantry.

If you would rather not use wine in this or any recipe, substitute apple juice or white grape juice. The dish will be a lot sweeter but still very good.

French Onion Soup

3 tablespoons butter	½ teaspoon sugar	6 slices French bread
1 tablespoon olive oil	8 cups Beef Stock (page 73)	1 tablespoon olive oil
5 yellow onions, thinly sliced	3 tablespoons all-purpose flour	3 tablespoons brandy
1 teaspoon salt	½ cup dry white wine	1½ cups grated Swiss cheese
	Salt and pepper to taste	

1. In a large sauté pan over medium heat, melt the butter with the oil. Add the onions and cover; sweat for 15 minutes, stirring occasionally. Uncover and add the salt and sugar. Cook over medium heat for 30 to 40 minutes, or until the onions are a dark golden brown. Stir occasionally; and do not have the heat too high; if the onions burn, they become bitter. In a saucepan, heat the stock until it simmers. When the onions are really brown, stir in the flour and cook for 1 minute. Pour in the hot stock and wine and taste for salt and pepper. Simmer for 30 minutes more, partially covered.

2. Brush one side of the French bread with olive oil and place under the broiler to lightly brown.

3. Just before serving, add the brandy to the pot and stir in 1/2 cup cheese. Spoon into oven-proof crocks, place toasted bread on top, sprinkle with Swiss cheese and then place under the broiler to melt the cheese. Or, put the croutons on a baking sheet, top with the cheese and place under the broiler to melt the cheese. Float one of these cheese croutons on the top of your soup. This soup freezes well.

[SERVES 6]

Gazpacho with Shellfish

4 ripe tomatoes, skinned, seeded and chopped
1 (13-ounce) can Italian tomatoes in juice
1 small white onion, chopped
2 cloves garlic, crushed
½ English cucumber, peeled, seeded and chopped
1 red bell pepper, seeded and chopped
1 cup tomato juice
½ cup extra virgin olive oil
¼ cup cider vinegar
Salt and pepper to taste
18 mussels
12 cooked shrimp
Chopped parsley for garnish

1. In a large nonmetallic bowl, combine the tomatoes, onion, garlic, cucumber, bell pepper, tomato juice, olive oil and vinegar. In a food processor, puree half the mixture until smooth. Add the remaining mixture and pulse 2 to 3 times to blend. The ideal texture is quite chunky. You may have to process this in batches. Season to taste and chill thoroughly.

2. To cook the mussels, put them in a saucepan with 1/4 cup water, cover with a tight-fitting lid and place over medium-high heat to cook. As soon as they open their shells, take them off the heat and cool. Discard any mussels that have not opened. If the shrimp need to be cooked, sauté them in a little olive oil just until they turn pink.

3. Spoon the chilled soup into bowls, arrange three mussels and two shrimp in each bowl and sprinkle with parsley.

[**SERVES 6**]

This is one of the favorite soups at the cooking school. After tasting this, students make fish stock! You can add any kind of shellfish to this recipe, and mussels and clams are also a nice addition.

Seafood Soup with Garlic Aioli

2 tablespoons olive oil
1 large onion, finely chopped
1 carrot, peeled and finely diced
2 cloves garlic, minced
¾ teaspoon turmeric
⅛ teaspoon cayenne pepper
1 teaspoon salt
Few grinds fresh pepper
½ cup dry white wine
8 cups Fish Stock (page 72)
2 tomatoes, chopped

½ teaspoon fennel seed, ground in a mortar and pestle
½ teaspoon dried thyme
1 large bay leaf
1 French bread baguette
Olive oil
1 pound snapper fillets, cut into 1-inch dice
1 pound cod fillets, cut into 1-inch dice
1 pound shrimp, shelled, tails left on

AIOLI

3 cloves garlic
½ teaspoon salt
1 whole egg
1 egg yolk
1 teaspoon Dijon mustard
1 cup extra virgin olive oil
¾ cup vegetable oil
1 teaspoon lemon juice

1. Heat the olive oil in a soup pot. Add the onion and carrot and cook, stirring occasionally, for 10 minutes. Add the garlic and cook for about 2 minutes. Add the turmeric, cayenne, salt and pepper and stir. Pour in the wine and boil for 1 minute. Add the stock, tomatoes, ground fennel seed, thyme, and bay leaf. Bring to a boil and then lower the heat to medium. Simmer, covered, for 30 minutes.
2. Slice the bread into 1/2-inch-thick slices, brush each side with olive oil and toast under the broiler.

3. In the last 5 minutes of cooking time add the seafood. Taste for salt (it often needs more).
4. Serve the soup in bowls topped with a toasted baguette slice and a teaspoon full of Aioli in the center of the toast.
5. For the Aioli, pound the garlic and the salt together with a mortar and pestle. Put it into a food processor bowl along with the egg, egg yolk and mustard. Turn the machine on and add the oils in a very slow steady stream. This will come to a thick emulsion. Add the lemon juice. This will keep in the refrigerator for about 5 days.

[SERVES 6 AS A MAIN COURSE OR 8 AS A STARTER]

This is a creamy soup perfect for the fall. Serve it with Stilton Biscuits (page 197).

Spiced Butternut Squash Soup

2   tablespoons butter
1   medium red onion, chopped
1   clove garlic, minced
1   teaspoon grated fresh ginger
¼   teaspoon garam masala

3   tablespoons all-purpose flour
1   teaspoon salt
½   teaspoon white pepper
3   cups Chicken Stock (page 72)
1½ pounds butternut squash,
      peeled, seeded and cut into
      ½-inch cubes

2   tablespoons dry sherry
1   tablespoon chopped chives
1   tablespoon chopped cilantro
cream to garnish

1. In a soup pot over medium heat, melt the butter until hot. Add the onion and cook for about 5 minutes. Add the garlic and ginger and cook for 1 minute. Stir in the garam masala, flour, salt and pepper. Cook for 1 minute. Add the stock and the squash, bring to a boil, cover and simmer for 10 minutes, or until the squash is soft. Add the sherry, chives and cilantro and then puree the soup in batches in a food processor or blender.

2. Serve garnished with a swirl of cream. This soup will freeze.

HINT: Garam masala is a blend of dried spices, ground together and used in many Indian dishes. Here we use it as a flavorful seasoning.

[SERVES 6]

Chicken Stock

2 whole chickens or chicken pieces (about 5 pounds)
1 large carrot, sliced

1 leek, sliced and cleaned
1 large onion, quartered
1 stalk parsley

1 bay leaf
1 sprig fresh thyme
1 teaspoon salt

1. Put all the ingredients in a large pot with water to cover by 1 inch and bring to a boil. Skim any gray foam off the top, lower the heat and simmer for a minimum of 2 hours.
2. Strain out the solids, and refrigerate the stock to chill down and congeal the fat. Skim the fat off the top, bag and freeze the stock.

HINT: At Culinary Concepts, we put big pots of beef and chicken stock together last thing at night or first thing in the morning, bring them to a boil, partially cover the pot and turn the heat down to the lowest setting so the stock barely simmers—all day or all night.

HINT: The chicken meat usually has no flavor left; however, if it tastes all right to you, use it in a salad or soup along with a lot of other flavors.

[MAKES ABOUT 3 QUARTS]]

Fish Stock

2 to 3 pounds fish trimmings, heads, back bones, flesh
6 cups cold water
2 cups dry white wine

¼ cup white wine vinegar
2 onions, cut into pieces
2 carrots, peeled and sliced
4 stalks celery with leaves, roughly chopped

6 sprigs parsley
2 bay leaves
10 peppercorns
1 teaspoon salt

1. Put all the ingredients in a large pot with water to cover by 1 inch and bring to a boil. Skim any gray foam off the top, lower the heat and simmer for a minimum of 2 hours.
2. Strain out the solids, and refrigerate the stock to chill down and congeal the fat. Skim the fat off the top, bag and freeze the stock.

HINT: If you cannot find fish bones, use a whole trout, flounder, sole or other mild-flavored fish fillets.

[MAKES ABOUT 3 QUARTS]

This is one stock that is really worth making. It is so hard to find a commercially made fish stock that is really good. I like to use a small salmon head or bones along with other fish to sweeten up my fish stocks.

Beef stock, sometimes referred to as brown stock, is the basis for many soups and sauces. It is rich and easy to make and it also makes your kitchen smell good!

Beef Stock

4 to 5 pounds beef bones, some with meat left on	2 stalks celery, plus any leaves, roughly chopped	1 bay leaf
2 onions, with skin, roughly quartered,	2 cloves garlic, smashed with a knife	2 sprigs chopped thyme or ¼ teaspoon dried thyme
2 to 3 carrots, scrubbed and roughly chopped	2 tomatoes, beyond their prime (optional)	10 peppercorns, smashed
	2 sprigs parsley, stems and leaves	1 tablespoon tomato paste
		1 teaspoon salt

1. Preheat the oven to 450 degrees F.

2. Put the beef bones in a large roasting pan and bake for 30 minutes. Add the onions, carrots, celery, garlic and tomatoes. Cook until browned, about 15 minutes.

3. Transfer all the roasted ingredients to a large stockpot. Add a little water to the roasting pan, put over medium heat and bring to a boil, scraping all the flavorful brown pieces off the bottom (this is called "deglazing the pan"). Pour into the stockpot. Add all the remaining ingredients and cover with cold water. Bring to a boil, and then reduce the heat to a simmer, skimming foam from the top of the stock if any has risen. Simmer slowly for 5 hours or overnight. Do not completely cover; the lid should have plenty of venting space. The stock should evaporate from the original scum line about 1 1/2 inches. Cool for about 1 hour and then carefully remove and discard the solids. (If you have a dog they will love the bones and flavorless meat). Strain the stock through a fine strainer into a large bowl and refrigerate until cold. This will congeal the fat so you can skim it off before packaging your stock and freezing it.

HINT: Use soup bones plus short ribs or some sort of cheap bones with some meat still on them. Traditionally stock was made from vegetables that were past their prime, so you went through your fridge to look for limp carrots and celery. The quantities you use of each ingredient is not too important. The more carrots you use, the sweeter your stock will be.

HINT: Do not completely cover stocks as they cook so they can evaporate down. The more gelatinous your stock is, the better the stock. When you freeze stock, do so by sealing it in a bag and placing it on a baking sheet with sides (if the bag leaks, the liquid is contained) so the stock bags freeze flat for easier storage.

[MAKES ABOUT 4 TO 5 QUARTS]

Vegetable Stock

3 medium carrots, peeled and cut into pieces	3 stalks celery with leaves, cut into pieces	1 bay leaf
3 medium onions, peeled and quartered	3 tomatoes, cut in half	1 teaspoon salt
	1 clove garlic, smashed	6 peppercorns
	6 sprigs parsley	6 cups cold water

1. Place all the ingredients in a stockpot. Bring to a boil and skim off any foam that rises to the top. Reduce the heat to medium-low (the stock should bubble around the edge) and simmer for 2 hours. Cool down and strain out the vegetables. Bag the stock and freeze.

HINT: If you want to sweeten a dish or stock, add more carrots. If you over-salted a soup or stew, add a peeled potato to absorb some of the salt.

[MAKES 6 CUPS]

Tropical Fruit Gazpacho

1½ cups tomato juice	¾ cup diced English cucumber (peeled and seeded)	⅓ teaspoon salt
1½ cups pineapple juice		1½ teaspoons bottled sweet chile sauce
¾ cup diced mango	⅓ cup diced green bell pepper	
¾ cup diced papaya	⅓ cup diced red bell pepper	Crème fraîche (or sour cream) and cilantro leaves to garnish
½ cup diced fresh pineapple	2 tablespoons chopped cilantro	

1. In a nonmetallic bowl, combine all the ingredients except garnish. Measure out 1 cup and set aside. Pour the rest of the gazpacho into the bowl of a food processor or blender and puree until smooth. Pour back into the bowl, add the reserved cup of diced gazpacho and chill for at least 2 hours.

2. Serve in individual bowls garnished with a spoonful of crème fraîche or a swirl of sour cream and a cilantro leaf.

HINT: Crème fraîche is used a lot in Europe. It is a slightly soured heavy cream. Sour cream is a good substitute.

[SERVES 6]

A cool, fresh soup that is quick to make. I always recommend using tomato juice that comes in a glass or plastic container.

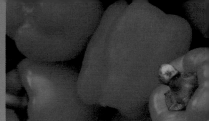

Roasted Red Pepper and Chile Soup

8 large red bell peppers
3 tablespoons butter
2 medium onions, chopped

10 cups Chicken Stock (page 72)
1 red chile, seeded and chopped
4 anchovy fillets

4 bay leaves
Salt and pepper to taste
6 tablespoons cream, divided

1. Preheat the broiler.
2. Cut the peppers in half, remove the seeds and white ribs and flatten. Place the peppers skin side up on a baking sheet. Slit ends with a knife to flatten. Place under the broiler until the skin really blackens. Put into a plastic bag for 10 minutes to sweat, and then easily peel off the skin. Slice skinned peppers into strips.

3. In a soup pot, melt the butter and sauté the onions until transparent. Add the skinned pepper strips and sauté lightly. Add the Chicken Stock, chile, anchovy and bay leaves; season with salt and pepper to taste. Simmer for 15 minutes.
4. Blend the soup in a food processor or blender until smooth. Stir in 4 tablespoons cream, adjust the seasoning and serve hot or chilled, garnished with a swirl of the remaining cream. This soup freezes well.

[SERVES 8 TO 10]

Fresh Berry Soup

1 (16-ounce) bag frozen
   raspberries
1 (16-ounce) bag frozen
   boysenberries

¾ cup light red wine, rose wine or
   cran/raspberry juice, divided
4 tablespoons honey
1½ cups sour cream, divided

2 cups chilled water
Mint sprigs to garnish

1. In a food processor, puree the berries and push through a strainer to remove the seeds. In a small saucepan, add half the wine and the honey. Heat just to dissolve the honey. Cool and stir into the berry puree along with the remain-ing wine, 3/4 cup sour cream and the cold water. Stir well and chill for several hours.
2. Serve in soup bowls with a swirl of sour cream in the center and a sprig of mint.

[SERVES 6]

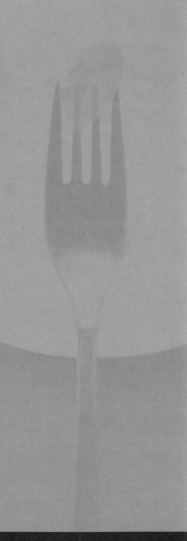

Salads

Salads should be attractive and inviting. I like to teach students to make salads on a platter rather than tossed in a bowl—they look more attractive and the heavier ingredients do not fall to the bottom of the bowl. Tuck leaves of fresh herbs among your salad greens—they add so much flavor. Dressings should be light and flavorful. There are wonderful flavored vinegars being sold that only need a little oil mixed with them to make a great vinaigrette.

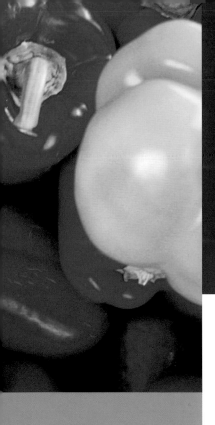

How To Shop And Store Your Groceries

Make an organized shopping list for the week (or for a special dinner) and only buy what is on your list. Shop the perimeters of a grocery store to avoid unnecessary purchases—the center aisles are filled with processed foods and those impulse-packaged foods that sit in your pantry or on your hips!

When you bring your groceries home, spend a few minutes preparing them for storage. Look over these tips for some great storage ideas:

• Take the wire twist off all vegetables. For lettuce, wash and spin it dry. I like to store my lettuce in the spinner.

• Fresh herbs should be washed and the stems put into a glass full of water (change the water every three days). Cover the top of the herb bunch with a plastic bag and refrigerate (except basil which should not be refrigerated). Your fresh herbs will last much longer stored this way.

• DO NOT refrigerate tomatoes or potatoes. The cold takes away all their flavor.

• Eggs that have spots of farm-yard dirt on them should be washed in a bowl of water with 1 teaspoon of bleach, then put into a cleaned refrigerator storage container.

• Fish should be unwrapped, put onto a clean plate, covered with plastic wrap and set over a bowl of ice or a frozen ice pack. DO NOT wash your fish until right before you cook it.

• Unwrap any meat wrapped in butcher paper, put onto a clean plate and cover with plastic wrap.

• Always store packages of meat on a tray or in a container that will not allow raw juices to drip onto other food.

• Flour, sugar and ingredients that make a mess when spilled should be stored in a sealed, labeled container.

This is a mildly spicy dressing. You can use 2 cans of sliced water chestnuts for the jicama, which is a large, brown-skinned root vegetable very popular in the Southwest.

Avocado, Jicama and Orange Salad

DRESSING
¼ cup orange juice
½ teaspoon salt
¼ teaspoon ground cumin
1 teaspoon ground ancho chile powder

2 tablespoons lime juice
4 tablespoons extra virgin olive oil

SALAD
3 navel oranges
1 medium jicama (about 1 pound)

2 cups lettuce, any kind, torn into bite-sized pieces
2 ripe avocados, sliced
1 cup sweet dried cranberries
Parsley sprigs

1. Whisk all the dressing ingredients together and set aside. This makes more dressing than you need for the salad, so use only as much as you need.

2. With a sharp knife, cut the peel and the white pith from the oranges. Working over a bowl, cut the orange sections free from the membranes. Peel the jicama and julienne slice into 2-inch-long pieces. Toss with a little dressing.

3. Place the lettuce on a platter, toss with a little dressing. Arrange the orange slices, jicama and avocado on top of the lettuce. Garnish with the sweet cranberries and parsley sprigs.

[SERVES 6]

This salad is a light, fragrant start to any meal.
If using bay scallops, cook them just until they lose their translucency.

Scallop and Butter Lettuce Salad with Ginger-Lime Dressing

1 cup walnut halves
1 pound sea scallops
Salt and pepper
1 teaspoon chopped fresh dill
2 tablespoons butter

1 head butter lettuce

DRESSING

2 teaspoons grated lime zest
½ cup lime juice
3 tablespoons extra virgin olive oil

2½ tablespoons honey
2 teaspoons grated fresh gingerroot
½ teaspoon salt
Pinch of white pepper

1. Preheat the oven to 350 degrees F.
2. To get rid of the rancid taste of walnut skins, bring a small saucepan of water to a boil and add the walnuts for about 30 seconds. Drain, put the walnuts on a baking sheet and then in the oven at 350 degrees F to dry, about 5 minutes.
3. Dry the scallops on a paper towel, sprinkle with salt, pepper and dill. In a medium-sized fry-ing pan melt the butter and sauté the scallops a few at a time, turning once, about 1 minute on each side. Put on a plate and chill in the refriger-ator.
4. Combine all the dressing ingredients and whisk well.
5. Wash and spin dry the lettuce, tear into bite-sized pieces and place on six individual salad plates. Top the lettuce with the scallops and walnuts; drizzle with the dressing.

[SERVES 6]

A quick and simple dressing to put together.

Simple Vinaigrette

½ teaspoon Dijon mustard
2 tablespoons flavored vinegar

½ cup vegetable or extra virgin
   olive oil or a mixture of both

Salt and pepper to taste
Honey to smooth, if necessary

1. In a small bowl combine the mustard and vinegar. Whisking well, slowly add the oil. Season with salt and pepper. If the vinaigrette is a little tart, smooth it out with a drop of honey. Always dress your salad lightly and serve extra vinaigrette on the side.

[MAKES 1/2 CUP]

Arugula, Avocado and Prosciutto Salad

DRESSING
2 teaspoons chopped shallot
1 clove garlic, crushed
3 tablespoons black fig vinegar
   (or a vinegar of your choice)

⅓ cup olive oil
Salt and pepper

SALAD
1 bag arugula (about 6 cups)
2 cups snow peas, trimmed and
   cut in half into 2-inch pieces

2 ripe avocados, peeled, pitted
   and sliced
6 slices prosciutto, each slice cut
   into 6 pieces
2 ounces chilled goat cheese,
   sliced

1. For the dressing, mix together the shallot, garlic, vinegar, oil, salt and pepper. Arrange the salad ingredients on a plate and drizzle with the dressing.

HINT: Do not dress your salad until just before serving. If you think that all the salad is not going to be used, pass the dressing. Undressed salad will keep if well covered and refrigerated.

[SERVES 6]

If you cannot find arugula you can substitute baby spinach or mâche.

This is a main dish salad. Serve this with Chile-Corn Sticks (page 194) and you will have a wonderful meal.

Southwestern Salad

6 cups torn lettuce
1 (4-ounce) can chopped green chiles
¼ cup vinaigrette or Italian salad dressing
Guacamole (page 59)

TOPPINGS
3 chicken breasts, cooked and shredded
1 cup grated longhorn cheese
2 hard-boiled eggs, quartered
2 carrots, peeled and cut into 2-inch sticks

2 stalks celery, cut into 2-inch sticks
1 bunch radishes, made into radish flowers
Black olives and small hot pickled peppers
Parsley to garnish

1. Toss together the lettuce, chiles and dressing and then spread out onto a platter. Top the salad with the chicken and spread Guacamole over the chicken. Sprinkle the cheese over the guacamole and decorate the salad with the remaining ingredients.

QUICK TIP: Substitute a store-bought cooked chicken and ready-made guacamole.
Radish flowers can be made using a paring knife to sculpt leaves around the radish or there is a gadget available that makes radish flowers.

[SERVES 8]

Sonoran Spinach Salad

DRESSING
½ cup chorizo sausage
3 green onions, finely chopped
3 cloves garlic, minced
¼ cup olive oil
¼ cup vegetable oil
2 tablespoons flavored vinegar
½ teaspoon sugar

¼ teaspoon salt
few grinds black pepper

CROUTONS
¼ cup olive oil
1 cup ½-inch French bread cubes
¼ teaspoon chipotle chile powder

SALAD
1 cup thinly sliced red onions
2 cups boiling water
6 cups well-washed baby spinach, stems removed
½ cup crumbled queso fresco to garnish

1. For the dressing, cook the chorizo in a pan over medium-high heat for about 2 minutes. Add the green onions and garlic, cook for 3 minutes and then drain onto a paper towel to absorb any grease.

2. For a hot dressing, return to the pan and add the rest of the dressing ingredients. Pour over salad and serve immediately. If you prefer a cold dressing, combine the dressing ingredients and serve over or beside the salad.

3. For the croutons, heat the olive oil in a frying pan until hot. Add the croutons and sauté, shak-ing the pan now and then until browned and crispy. Toss with the chile powder and set aside.

4. Put the onions in a strainer and run the boil-ing water over them to partially wilt. Plunge into ice cold water to chill down; pat dry. Mix the spinach and onions in a bowl, pour on the hot dressing, toss, spoon onto salad plates and top with the croutons and queso fresco. Serve at once.

[SERVES 6]

If pomegranate seeds are out of season, substitute raspberries or sweet dried cranberries.

Baby Greens with Pomegranate Seeds and Spiced Pecans

PECANS

3   tablespoons unsalted butter
¼   cup light brown sugar
1   tablespoon water
1½ teaspoons chili powder
¾   teaspoon salt
½   teaspoon ground cumin
½   teaspoon dried oregano
¼   teaspoon ground black pepper

Pinch of cayenne pepper
4   cups pecans

DRESSING

⅓   cup extra virgin olive oil
1   tablespoon lemon juice
1   tablespoon thawed frozen
     orange juice concentrate
¼   teaspoon kosher salt

¼   teaspoon freshly ground pepper

SALAD

¼   cup thinly sliced red onion
1   cup boiling water
3   oranges or red grapefruit
8   cups baby greens
1   cup crumbled soft goat cheese
¼   cup pomegranate seeds

1.   Preheat oven to 300 degrees F.

PECANS

2.   Spray a baking sheet with nonstick spray or use a silicone pan liner. In a large sauté pan over medium heat, melt the butter. Add the sugar and stir gently until dissolved. Take off the heat and add the remaining ingredients. Stir until the nuts are well coated. Spread the mixture onto the prepared baking sheet and put into the oven. Cook for about 25 minutes, stirring often. The nuts need to be glazed and a rich brown color; cool completely. These will keep in an airtight container for about 10 days.

DRESSING

3.   Whisk the oil, lemon juice, orange juice, salt and pepper in a bowl and set aside.

SALAD

4.   Put the onion slices in a strainer and pour the boiling water over them. Run them under cold water to refresh and dry them on a paper towel. This eliminates some of the strong onion flavor. Cut the peel and the pith from the oranges. Cut in half and slice into 1/4-inch slices. Spread the baby greens out on a large platter, arrange the orange/grapefruit slices around the side. Sprinkle the top with the goat cheese and red onion. Top with the pecans and pomegranate seeds; drizzle with the dressing. Serve immediately.

HINT: Fresh pomegranates are available during the winter months. One pomegranate should give you 1/2 cup. To open a pomegranate, score around the fruit with a sharp knife and twist it to open. Hold the open side towards a bowl and hit the top with the back of a kitchen knife. The seeds should pop out. The juice really stains so be careful where you splatter it. Many stores now sell the seeds fresh or frozen in packages.

[SERVES 8]

You can change this salad by using a different berry and a
different nut. If Stilton cheese is not available, use any blue cheese.

Pear, Endive and Stilton Salad

DRESSING
½ teaspoon Dijon mustard
1 shallot, very finely chopped
1 whole star anise, crushed with
  a mortar and pestle
3 tablespoons orange juice
1 tablespoon port wine

⅓ cup vegetable oil

SALAD
2 ripe pears, without bruises
1 lemon, juiced
2 heads Belgian endive
3 cups baby greens

4 ounces Stilton cheese, crumbled
½ cup blueberries
¼ cut pine nuts, toasted in a dry pan
Fresh parsley to garnish

1. To make the dressing, whisk together the mustard, shallot, star anise, orange juice and port. Whisking well, slowly drizzle in the oil. Set aside. This can be made ahead.
2. Cut the pears in half, core and slice. Sprinkle with a little lemon juice to stop them going brown. Slice the stalk end of the endive off to separate the leaves. Wash and spin dry. Place the greens on a plate and tuck the endive spears around the edges. Arrange the pear slices on top and sprinkle with the crumbled Stilton cheese, blueberries and pine nuts. Drizzle with the dressing and garnish with parsley. This salad can be made on individual plates or on one large platter.

[SERVES 6]

Basic Vinaigrette Dressing

1 small shallot, finely chopped
⅓ cup flavored vinegar
¾ teaspoon Dijon mustard

2 tablespoons finely chopped
  Italian parsley
¼ teaspoon salt
Few grinds of pepper

⅓ cup vegetable oil
⅓ cup extra virgin olive oil
Honey to sweeten, if necessary

1. In a small bowl mix together the shallot, vinegar, mustard, parsley, salt and pepper. Drizzle in the oils, whisking well. Use a piece of lettuce to taste for seasoning. Depending on the vinegar used, the dressing may need more salt or a bit of honey.

[MAKES 1 CUP]

This is a basic recipe. You can change the flavor by changing the
vinegar flavor, the fresh herbs you use and adding some garlic.

Seafood

For me, seafood was a childhood staple (along with lamb). We would catch and clean or buy fish whole and fillet them ourselves before cooking. I find students are cautious about cooking seafood, mostly because they tend to overcook and dry it out. Fish is very versatile. I instruct my students to shop for the freshest fish available and not feel that they can only use the type of fish the recipe calls for.

Seafood Tips

Buying Fish

Fish should be sweet smelling and glossy. If it smells really fishy and looks dry, do not buy it. Once you've purchased fish, it should be used within 24 hours. When you get the fish home, take it out of the wrapper, place it on a plate over a bowl of ice (make sure the plate is larger than the bowl, you do not want your fish drowning in melted ice water). Cover with plastic wrap. For live seafood like mussels or clams, make sure they can breath, so do not cover with plastic. We like to pack frozen gel packs around them in the refrigerator to keep them cold.

When buying frozen seafood, make sure it is still frozen when you buy it. Do not buy freshly defrosted seafood because you do not know how long ago it was defrosted. Take the fish home and defrost it yourself by putting it in a sealed plastic bag and running cold water over it. Frozen fish will be dryer than fresh fish and the flesh will have a different texture.

Cooking Fish

If you feel you have to wash fish, do so just before it is cooked. I never wash fish. To test if fish is cooked through, put two forks back to back at the thickest part and gently pull away the flesh. The top layer of the fish should pull away easily with slight resistance in the center—think of a medium-cooked steak. By the time the fish is plated and on the table, the fish will be perfectly cooked through.

Shrimp should be cooked just until they turn pink. Fresh mussels and clams should be tightly closed. Any that have opened and will not close when tapped have died and should be discarded. Cook the shellfish just until they open, and discard those that do not open in the allotted cooking time.

Broiled Fish with Shrimp, and Mango and Avocado Salsa

12 shrimp, peeled and deveined
1 tablespoon olive oil
1 tablespoon lime juice
¼ teaspoon chipotle chile powder
Vegetable oil
Salt and pepper
4 pieces fish (Cabrilla, sea bass, halibut), about 1 pound total

SALSA
¼ teaspoon lime zest
2 teaspoons lime juice
½ teaspoon orange zest
½ avocado, chopped into medium dice
1 tablespoon minced cilantro
½ teaspoon chipotle chile in

adobo sauce
½ cup medium-diced mango
Pinch of cinnamon
Pinch of nutmeg
Salt and pepper to taste

Menu suggestions
Tropical Fruit Gazpacho
(page 74)

Pear, Endive
and Stilton Salad
(page 89)

Lemon Risotto with Basil
(page 136)

Brandied Apple Mousse
(page 219)

Wine suggestion
Champagne, Sparkling
Wine, Pinot Gris or
Pinot Grigio

Sparkling White
Grape Juice

1. Marinate the shrimp in the olive oil, lime juice and chile powder for 15 minutes. Gently mix all the salsa ingredients together and set aside.
2. Preheat the broiler. Brush a baking sheet with vegetable oil. Salt and pepper the fish. Remove the shrimp from the marinade and place both the shrimp and the fish on the baking sheet. Place under the broiler, turning the shrimp as soon as they turn pink and removing them from the pan as soon as both sides are cooked. Turn the fish over after 3 minutes. Broil the fish until just done when tested with two forks as explained in the introduction of this chapter (page 90). Do not overcook.
3. Serve the fish topped with the shrimp and a spoonful of the salsa on the side.

[SERVES 4]

Poached Salmon with Caviar Béarnaise

4 medium salmon steaks or 1½
  pounds salmon fillet
2 sprigs dill
1 small onion, sliced
3 cups water
1 cup white wine
½ teaspoon each salt and pepper

CAVIAR BEARNAISE

2 egg yolks
½ cup unsalted butter, cut into
  slices
1 teaspoon lemon juice
3 tablespoons white wine
¼ cup tarragon white wine vinegar

3 cracked peppercorns
1 small bay leaf
Pinch of dried chervil
1 ounce red lumpfish caviar
  (comes in a 2-ounce jar)

Menu suggestions

Spinach Ravioli with Chile-
Tomato Cream Sauce
(page 50)

Lemon Risotto with Basil
(page 136)

Frozen Lemon
Soufflé Cake
(page 221)

Wine suggestions

Pinot Gris or Pinot Grigio

1. Place the salmon in a deep frying pan or wok and cover with the remaining ingredients. Bring to a boil and then lower the heat so it simmers gently for about 8 minutes for the steaks or 5 minutes for the fillet. Fish is cooked when you test it with two forks, carefully pulling apart the flesh, it should come apart easily. It is better to undercook fish than to overcook it. Once cooked, carefully lift out of the pan onto a serving dish. Discard the onion and dill, strain the liquid and freeze to use as fish stock.

CAVIAR BEARNAISE

2. For the béarnaise, add the egg yolks and a slice of butter to a small saucepan. Whisk over very low heat until the butter has melted. Be careful, if the heat gets too high you will scramble the eggs. Keep adding slices of butter until you have whisked it all into the egg yolks. You should have a nice creamy sauce. Add the lemon juice.

3. In a very small saucepan, combine the wine, vinegar, peppercorns, bay leaf and chervil. Bring to a boil and lower the heat to medium; cook to reduce the liquid to 1 tablespoon. Strain the liquid into the egg mixture. Very carefully fold in the caviar. If you need to keep this sauce for longer than about 15 minutes, pour it into a wide-mouth thermos to keep warm. Serve the sauce with the salmon.

[SERVES 4]

This is a beautiful presentation and, with the help of frozen puff pastry, is very easy to put together. Use small canapé cutters to cut shapes out of leftover pastry to decorate the top, or let your imagination go and cut your own designs.

Salmon and Spinach in Puff Pastry

1½ pounds salmon fillet
Salt and pepper
1   (8-ounce) package baby spinach
¼   cup water
⅓   cup grated mozzarella cheese

½   cup ricotta cheese
Pinch of freshly grated nutmeg
2   green onions, chopped
1   tablespoon chopped chives
½   teaspoon salt
4   grinds fresh pepper

1   sheet frozen puff pastry, defrosted overnight in the refrigerator
1   egg yolk
1   tablespoon water

1.   Cut the salmon in half and lay together to make about a 12 inch length. Season lightly with salt and pepper; set aside.
2.   Wash the spinach well, put into a saucepan with 1/4 cup water and cook until just wilted, about 3 minutes. Plunge the spinach into a bowl of iced water, cool down, drain and squeeze out any water. Chop finely and put into a medium mixing bowl. Stir in the mozzarella and ricotta cheese, add the nutmeg, green onions, chives, salt and pepper.
3.   On a floured board, roll out one sheet of the puff pastry to approximately 8 x 13 inches.
4.   Lay the salmon down the center of half the pastry, leaving an inch on each side of the salmon. Cut in half making sure the other half is slightly larger than the bottom half.

5.   Carefully spread the top of the salmon with the spinach mixture. Mix together the egg yolk and the water to form an egg wash. Brush the egg wash around the bottom perimeter of the pastry. Roll the other half of the pastry out to be larger than the bottom. Drape the pastry over the salmon and with a fork press the edges together. Cut off any excess pastry to use as a decoration. Brush the pastry with the egg wash, decorate and refrigerate for 30 minutes before cooking.
6.   Preheat the oven to 400 degrees F. Cook the salmon pastry for 15 to 20 minutes or until the pastry is crisp and golden brown.

[SERVES 6]

Menu suggestions

Roasted Red Pepper and Chile Soup
(page 75)

Green Bean and Carrot Bundles
(page 146)

Buttermilk Panna Cotta
(page 209)

Wine suggestions

White Burgundy or a French Style Chardonnay

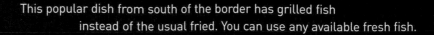
This popular dish from south of the border has grilled fish instead of the usual fried. You can use any available fresh fish.

Grilled Fish Tacos with Tropical Fruit Salsa

1 pound fish, such as cod, Cabrilla or swordfish, cut into ½ x 2-inch strips

2 teaspoons seafood seasoning (Cajun Seafood Seasoning, Seafood Magic)

8 corn tortillas
4 cups shredded green cabbage
Tropical Fruit Salsa (page 160)

Menu suggestions

Red Bean and
Pineapple Rice
(page 122)

Chocolate-Chile Ice Cream
with Poached Fruit Salsa
(pages 214, 208)

Wine suggestions

Sauvignon Blanc, Fume
Blanc or Pinot Gris

Mexican Beer

1. Sprinkle the fish with the seasoning and grill in a grill pan over medium-high heat until just cooked. Do not overcook.
2. Warm the tortillas, wrapped in foil, in the oven. Place 2 tortillas on a plate, fill with 1/4 of the fish, top with shredded cabbage and fold over. Serve with Fruit Salsa on the side.
3. Salsa will keep for 4 days.

[SERVES 4]

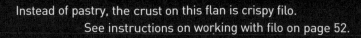

Instead of pastry, the crust on this flan is crispy filo.
See instructions on working with filo on page 52.

Filo Seafood Flan

CRUST
½ cup butter, melted
8 (9 x 14-inch) sheets filo dough

FILLING
¼ cup water
¼ cup dry white wine
½ pound crabmeat, shrimp or bay
scallops, or a mixture of them
¼ pound white fish fillet
¼ teaspoon lemon juice
3 eggs
½ cup whipping cream
¼ teaspoon salt
¼ teaspoon pepper
2 teaspoons chopped parsley
1 cup grated Swiss cheese

Menu suggestions

Gazpacho with Shellfish
(page 66)

Avocado, Jicama and
Orange Salad
(page 78)

Brandied Apple Mousse
(page 219)

Wine suggestions

A new-world style
Chardonnay

CRUST

1. Using a small pastry brush, brush the inside of the (8½-inch) quiche pan with 1½- to 2-inch-high sides, with melted butter. One by one, butter each sheet of filo and gently lay them in the deep quiche pan. Trim the edges of overlapping filo with scissors and tuck them under to make a smooth edge. Place in the freezer to set the butter.

2. Preheat the oven to 400 degrees F. In a small frying pan, bring the water and the wine to a simmer. Add crabmeat (if uncooked), shrimp or bay scallops and fish. Poach for about 3 minutes. Remove the seafood and save 1/4 cup of the poaching water. Flake the fish and chop the shrimp. Mix with the lemon juice.

3. In a bowl, beat the eggs with the cream, 1/4 cup of reserved poaching liquid, salt and pepper. Place the quiche pan on a baking sheet. Sprinkle the seafood over the bottom of the filo crust, top with the parsley and cheese. Carefully pour the egg mixture over the top.

4. Bake for 20 to 25 minutes, or until the center is firm to the touch but not beginning to rise. Allow to sit for 10 minutes before taking out of the pan and slicing.

[SERVES 6 AS A LUNCHEON DISH]

Tamarind is the tart sticky pulp from the pods of the tamarind shade tree. It is a popular flavoring in Mexican and Asian foods.

Fish with Macadamia Nut Crust and Tamarind Cream Sauce

6   portions fresh white fish, such as Cabrilla, sea bass or halibut (about 1½ pounds)
½   cup buttermilk
1   cup macadamia nuts, finely chopped in a food processor
4   tablespoons vegetable oil

SAUCE
1   tablespoon tamarind paste (not concentrate)
½   cup boiling water
1   tablespoon vegetable oil
1   small shallot, chopped
½   teaspoon minced garlic

1   teaspoon chopped fresh ginger
1   small red chile, finely chopped
½   cup coconut cream
Salt and pepper to taste
2   tablespoons chopped cilantro to garnish

1.   Dip the fish into the buttermilk and then roll in the macadamia nuts. In a medium non-stick pan over medium heat, heat the oil until hot. Add the fish and sauté until browned on one side. Turn over and cook until the other side is browned and the fish is just cooked through; keep warm.

SAUCE
2.   Soak the tamarind paste in the boiling water, turn off the heat for 15 minutes. Strain through a fine sieve and press on the pulp to extract all of the flavor. In the same pan the fish was cooked in, heat the oil and add the shallot and garlic. Cook until the shallot has softened, about 3 minutes. Add the ginger and the chile; cook gently for about 2 minutes. Stir in the tamarind liquid and bring to a boil. Take off the heat and stir in the coconut cream. Taste for salt and pepper. Place the piece of fish on a serving platter, spoon sauce over top and garnish with cilantro.

[SERVES 6]

Menu suggestions

Spiced Butternut Squash Soup
(page 70)

Red Bean and Pineapple Rice
(page 122)

Pumpkin-Ginger Cheesecake
(page 215)

Wine suggestions

A dry Riesling
(Kabinett or Spatlese)

If possible, use wild salmon rather than farm-raised salmon as the flavor is better. You can also use shrimp cooked in the sauce.

Grilled Salmon with Linguini and Tomato-Dill Marinara

3   tablespoons olive oil
2   tablespoons lemon juice
1   teaspoon finely chopped fresh dill
1   pound skinless salmon fillet, cut into 4 pieces

SAUCE
1½ tablespoons olive oil
2   tablespoons shallots, finely chopped
1   clove garlic, finely chopped
1   (16-ounce) can good Italian tomatoes
½   cup Fish Stock (page 72) or clam juice
1   tablespoon tomato paste
1   tablespoon finely chopped fresh dill
1   tablespoon finely chopped Italian parsley
½   cup apple juice
1   bay leaf
Salt and pepper
8   ounces fresh or dried linguini
Chopped parsley to garnish

Menu suggestions

Pear, Endive
and Stilton Salad
(page 89)

Strawberry Tiramisu
(page 204)

Wine suggestions

Pinot Noir or a Zinfandel

1. Mix oil, lemon juice and dill together. Pour over the salmon and marinate in a non-metallic container for 30 minutes.
2. Preheat the broiler.
3. In a large sauté pan, make the sauce by heating the oil over medium heat. Sauté the shallots and garlic until tender. Crush the canned tomatoes and add them to the pan along with the stock, tomato paste, dill, parsley, apple juice and bay leaf. Simmer until the sauce is thick, about 20 minutes. Taste for salt and pepper. Remove the bay leaf.

4. Bring a large pot of water to a boil and add 1 teaspoon salt.
5. Put the salmon on a baking sheet, lightly salt and pepper and put under the broiler for 3 minutes on each side. Or, heat a grill pan to very hot on the stovetop to cook the salmon, turning once. Test with a fork to see if it is just cooked through.
6. Put the linguini into the salted boiling water and cook until it rises to the top of the pot. If you are using dried pasta it will take longer to cook.
7. Divide the pasta into four individual bowls, top with some of the sauce and a piece of the salmon, sprinkle with chopped parsley and serve.

[SERVES 4]

Sushi Class

1

2

1. Spread the sushi rice onto the nori, which has been placed on a bamboo rolling mat.

2. Use the rolling mat (makisu) to help roll the California roll.

3. Making sushi with friends.

4. Fill the California roll (Futomaki) with cucumber, avocado, crab and black sesame seeds.

5. Roll the mat away from you, pressing the ingredients with your finger to keep the roll firm.

6. The completed roll, ready for slicing and garnishing.

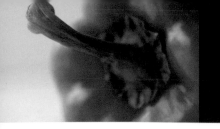

This is one of the favorite recipes in the cooking school. These can be prepared in advance and frozen before they are cooked. Partially defrost in the refrigerator overnight and then cook them at 350 degrees F for 30 minutes.

Filo-Wrapped Salmon with Roasted Red Pepper Sauce

1 leek
½ cup butter, divided
1 clove garlic
2 cups sliced mushrooms
4 cups fresh spinach
1 teaspoon salt
Few grinds of pepper

¼ teaspoon red pepper flakes
12 sheets filo
6 fillets salmon, 3 ounces each

ROASTED RED PEPPER SAUCE
2 red bell peppers
1 cup chicken stock

1 small white onion, chopped
5 cloves garlic, crushed
1 tablespoon red wine vinegar
2 tablespoons chopped fresh basil
Salt and pepper

Menu suggestions

Tropical Fruit Gazpacho
(page 74)

Green Beans with Cherry Tomatoes
(page 141)

Frozen Lemon Soufflé Cake
(page 221)

Wine suggestions

Pinot Noir

1. Trim the leek down to the white part and cut off the root. Split in half and wash well. Cut into matchstick strips. Melt 2 tablespoons butter in a frying pan and sauté the leeks over medium heat until soft, about 4 minutes. Add the garlic and cook for another minute. Add the mushrooms and cook until they are almost dry. Wash the spinach and add to the pan along with the salt, pepper and red pepper flakes. Cook just until the spinach is wilted. Turn out of the pan onto a dish to cool.
2. Heat the oven to 400 degrees F.
3. Melt the remaining butter. Place one filo sheet on a work surface. Brush quickly with a light coating of butter. Fold in half. Place one-sixth of the spinach mixture in the lower center of the filo, top with a piece of the salmon. Fold in the sides and roll up forming a rectangle. Brush the entire package with butter. Lay out a second piece of filo, brush with butter and fold in half. Place the wrapped salmon in the middle of the filo and wrap as shown in the photograph. Place on a baking sheet. Repeat 5 more times. Bake until the filo pastry is pale golden, about 20 minutes. Serve

with the Red Pepper Sauce.
4. To make the sauce, preheat the broiler. Slice the peppers in half, remove the stem, white veins and seeds. Place on a baking sheet under a hot broiler to char the skins. Place the peppers in a plastic bag to sweat for 10 minutes. Peel the skin from the peppers and set aside.
5. In a small saucepan, bring 1/2 cup chicken stock and the onion to a boil. Add the crushed garlic and lower the heat to medium. Cook until nearly all the liquid has evaporated.
6. In a food processor or blender, combine the onion mixture, red peppers, remaining chicken stock, red wine vinegar and basil. Blend until the mixture is smooth. Taste for salt and pepper. The sauce can be frozen at this stage, just reheat before serving.

HINT: This sauce freezes well and can also be used on roasted poultry.

[SERVES 6]

Rolled Soufflé with Seafood Filling

SOUFFLE
Butter to grease pan
2 cups milk
¼ cup butter
½ cup flour
4 eggs, separated
½ cup grated sharp cheddar
    cheese
½ cup grated Parmesan cheese
¼ teaspoon salt

SEAFOOD FILLING
2 tablespoons butter
6 green onions, chopped
2 cups sliced mushrooms
½ pound cooked scallops or
    shrimp
½ pound cooked crabmeat
1 (3-ounce) package cream
    cheese, softened
¼ cup sour cream
1 teaspoon lemon juice
2 drops Tabasco
½ teaspoon salt
Pinch of white pepper

Menu suggestions

Avocado, Jicama
and Orange Salad
(page 78)

Individual Frozen Lime
Cheesecakes
(page 224)

Wine suggestions

Champagne or Sparkling
Wine

1. Preheat the oven to 375 degrees F.
2. Prepare a 10 x 13-inch jellyroll pan by greasing it with butter and lining it with parchment paper. Grease the top of the paper.
3. In a small saucepan, scald the milk, being careful that it does not boil over. In a larger pot melt the butter, whisk in the flour and cook for 2 minutes. Whisking, gradually add the milk and cook until it boils and thickens. Remove from the heat and pour into a large bowl. Whisk the egg yolks together and gradually beat into the milk mixture. Stir in the cheddar cheese, 1/4 cup Parmesan cheese and salt.
4. Beat the egg whites until they are stiff and gently fold into the batter. Pour into the prepared pan and bake in the lower third of the oven for 30 to 35 minutes or until golden brown.
5. Have ready a slightly dampened kitchen towel and a sheet of parchment paper. When the soufflé is cooked, loosen the sides with a knife, sprinkle the top with the remaining Parmesan cheese, cover with the parchment paper and the damp towel and turn over. Remove the parchment paper from the bottom of the soufflé and spread the bottom with the filling. With the help of the towel, roll the soufflé up into a jellyroll lengthwise.
6. This can be refrigerated overnight and warmed through the next day. Cover with foil and place in a 375-degree F oven for 15 minutes or until hot.

SEAFOOD FILLING

7. Melt the butter in a medium frying pan, add the green onions and the mushrooms.
8. Cook until the mushrooms are almost dry. Remove from heat and put into a bowl. If the scallops are not cooked, melt 1 tablespoon butter in the pan and sauté them for about 3 minutes. Add to the onion mixture along with the crab, cream cheese, sour cream, lemon juice and Tabasco. Season with salt and pepper and taste to correct seasonings.

[SERVES 6]

This can be served as an appetizer, luncheon dish or as a main course. If you do not have individual ovenproof scallop shells or small dishes, you could make this in one large ovenproof platter and serve it family-style.

Coquilles St. Jacques

2 large baking potatoes, peeled and cut into 1-inch pieces
½ teaspoon salt
2 tablespoons melted butter
1 egg, beaten
¼ teaspoon white pepper
Salt to taste

2 tablespoons butter
3 tablespoons finely chopped shallot
1 clove garlic, minced
4 ounces sliced fresh mushrooms
1 cup Fish Stock (page 72) or ¾ cup water and ¼ cup white wine
1¼ pounds bay scallops
3 tablespoons butter

3 tablespoons flour
½ cup grated Swiss cheese
¼ teaspoon salt
White pepper to taste
3 tablespoons chopped parsley for garnish

Menu suggestions

French Onion Soup
(page 64)

Salad Greens
with Vinaigrette
(pages 82, 89)

Individual Frozen
Lime Cheesecakes
(page 224)

Wine suggestions

A dry Riesling (Kabinett
and Spatlese)

1. Place potatoes in a large pot, cover with water, add 1/2 teaspoon salt and bring to a boil, cover and lower the heat to a simmer. Cook until just tender, about 20 minutes; drain well. Mash through a potato ricer and add 2 tablespoons melted butter and the beaten egg. Add white pepper and salt if needed. Allow to cool to just warm. Put potato into a piping bag with a large star tip and pipe potato rosettes around the perimeter of 6 large scallop shells or ovenproof serving dishes.

2. In a medium frying pan, melt 2 tablespoons butter and sauté the shallots for 2 minutes. Add the garlic and sauté for a few seconds. Add the mushrooms and sauté until lightly browned.

3. In a small saucepan, bring the Fish Stock to a boil. Add the scallops and any juices, lower the heat to a simmer and poach the scallops until just cooked, about 2 minutes. Do not cook them too much or they will become tough. Strain, reserving 1 1/4 cups of the poaching liquid for the sauce.

4. Using the same saucepan, melt 3 tablespoons butter, add the flour and cook for 1 minute. Whisk in the warm poaching liquid and bring to a boil. Take pan off the heat and add Swiss cheese. Taste for salt and pepper. Add the mushroom mixture and scallops to the sauce and spoon the sauce into the center of the scallop shells. This dish can be done to this point and refrigerated for up to 24 hours.

5. Just before serving, place the shells under a hot broiler to brown the potatoes and heat the sauce through. Garnish with the parsley.

VARIATION: Use shrimp, fish, crab, mussels or a seafood combination to make this dish your own special creation.

[SERVES 6]

This is an unusual way of cooking fish. I made this for a wedding party of 50. It was easy to put together, cook in one oven and serve. The fish steams inside the plastic wrap. If you prefer, use parchment paper instead of the plastic wrap.

Crab-Stuffed Salmon Fillet

1 salmon fillet, about 2 to 3 pounds, skinned
1½ cups soy sauce
¾ cup sake
2 tablespoons freshly grated gingerroot

6 fresh shiitake mushrooms, cut into thin strips (or dried, soaked in warm water for 30 minutes)
1 small carrot, peeled and cut into matchsticks
½ small onion, cut into matchsticks

4 spears asparagus
¾ cup fresh or canned crabmeat
Extra cooked asparagus for garnish
Zest of 1 lemon to garnish

1. Butterfly the salmon fillet (slice almost through the salmon along the length so you can open it up like a book to almost double the width). In a large plastic bag, combine the soy sauce, sake and fresh ginger. Add the salmon and marinate in the refrigerator for 4 hours.
2. Preheat the oven to 350 degrees F.
3. Remove the salmon from the marinade. Place a large strip of plastic wrap on the work table and place the salmon fillet skinned side down and opened out ready to fill. Layer mushrooms, carrot, onion, asparagus spears and crab onto one side of the salmon. Bring the other side over the filling to enclose it. Using the plastic wrap to help (without rolling the wrap inside the fish), tightly roll the salmon in the plastic wrap jellyroll fashion and fold in the ends to seal. Wrap the salmon in the plastic in a layer of wide foil and seal well. Yes, it is sealed in plastic wrap and then in foil! Place on a baking sheet in the oven for 35 minutes.
4. Remove from the oven and remove the foil. Slice the salmon into serving pieces through the plastic. Remove the plastic once you have the slice of salmon on the serving plate. Garnish with the lemon zest and the cooked asparagus.

[SERVES 8]

Menu suggestions

Hot Goat Cheese
Soufflé with Arugula Salad
(page 38)

Lemon Risotto with Basil
(page 136)

Frozen Lemon Soufflé
Cake
(page 221)

Wine suggestions

A dry Gewurztraminer

Shrimp, Scallop and Orzo Sauté

1½ teaspoons salt, divided
1 cup orzo pasta
¼ cup butter, divided
½ pound asparagus
3 tablespoons oil
6 cloves garlic, minced

1 pound white button mushrooms, sliced
1 large tomato, skinned, seeded
   and chopped
2 tablespoons tomato paste
¼ cup white wine or apple juice

1 cup sliced green onions
¼ cup lemon juice
1 pound bay scallops
1 pound medium shrimp, shelled
   and deveined
½ cup chopped fresh parsley

Menu suggestions

Baby Greens with
Pomegranate Seeds and
Spiced Pecans
(page 88)

Green Bean and Carrot
Bundles
(page 146)

Frozen Lemon
Soufflé Cake
(page 221)

Wine suggestions

Sauvignon Blanc or a
Fume Blanc

1. Bring a large pot (about 4-quart size) full
of water to a boil. Add 1/2 teaspoon salt and
the orzo pasta. Cook the pasta until just
cooked, about 5 to 6 minutes. Drain and toss
with 1 tablespoon of the butter and 1/2 teaspoon salt; set aside.

2. Fill a medium saucepan with water and
bring to a boil. Break the ends off the asparagus and cut into 1-inch pieces. Add remaining
salt and the asparagus to the boiling water
and cook until just tender, 4 to 5 minutes.
Drain and plunge the asparagus into a bowl of
iced water. When cold, pat dry on a paper
towel.

3. In a large (12- to 14-inch) sauté pan, melt
3 tablespoons of butter and the oil over medium heat. Add the garlic and sauté for 1
minute. Add the mushrooms and increase the
heat to high. Cook until they soften and
release their juices, about 5 minutes. Add the
tomato, tomato paste and stir to blend. Add
the wine, green onions and lemon juice. Stir in
the scallops, shrimp and their juices. Cook for
3 minutes, or until the shrimp just turn pink.
Stir in the orzo and the asparagus; heat
through. Serve immediately in individual serving dishes or family-style in one large platter.
Sprinkle with the parsley.

[SERVES 6]

Starches

With every main course, it is usual to include a starch of some kind. Some of the starches in this chapter also include vegetables, which with a piece of meat or fish make a complete meal. Any recipe can be easily adapted for the vegetarian by using vegetable stock or water. Rice is the only starch I would freeze. In fact, I usually have small bags of plain cooked rice in the freezer that can be added to stir-fried vegetables for a quick dish. Orzo is a rice-shaped pasta that I like to buy from Middle Eastern stores. You cook it in plenty of boiling water like dried pasta and can serve it hot or at room temperature. Make sure you salt your starches well, as they tend to absorb salt and are rather tasteless if they are lacking in salt.

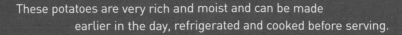

These potatoes are very rich and moist and can be made earlier in the day, refrigerated and cooked before serving.

Parmesan-Crusted Potatoes

3 cloves roasted garlic

1 teaspoon olive oil

2 pounds Yukon Gold potatoes, peeled and cut into 2-inch pieces

1 teaspoon salt

¼ cup cold milk

¼ cup unsalted butter, softened

Salt and white pepper

½ cup whipping cream

2 tablespoons butter, melted

½ cup freshly grated Parmesan cheese

1. Preheat oven to 400 degrees F.

2. Wrap the garlic and olive oil in a small piece of foil or put into a garlic roaster. Bake for 20 minutes until soft and golden brown.

3. Butter an 8 x 11-inch baking dish. Put the potatoes in a large saucepan and cover with water. Bring to a boil, add the salt, and then simmer until tender, about 15 minutes. Drain and return the potatoes to the saucepan and shake over high heat for 1 minute to dry. Pass the potatoes through a potato ricer into a large bowl, or mash well with a potato mash-er. Beat in the milk. Squeeze the roasted garlic cloves out of their skin and mash with the 1/4 cup butter. Add to the potatoes. Taste and season with salt and pepper.

4. With an electric mixer, beat the cream to soft peaks. Fold the cream into the potatoes. Scrape the potatoes into the prepared baking dish, drizzle with the melted butter and sprinkle with Parmesan cheese. Bake potatoes for 20 minutes. Preheat the broiler and broil the potatoes for 2 minutes until browned. Let stand for 10 minutes before serving.

[SERVES 6 TO 8]

Potato nests can also be filled with green peas, a mound of cooked spinach or cooked broccoli. They make a colorful presentation.

Potato Nests

3 large russet potatoes
1½ teaspoons salt
2 egg yolks
¼ cup milk or cream
¼ cup butter, melted
⅛ teaspoon white pepper

⅛ teaspoon grated nutmeg
3 ripe tomatoes, skinned and
   seeded
Salt and pepper
4 ounces feta cheese, crumbled

¼ cup chopped niçoise olives
2 tablespoons olive oil
1 egg yolk
1 tablespoon water
2 tablespoons chopped parsley
   for garnish

1. Peel the potatoes and cut into even pieces. Put the potatoes into a pot and cover with cold water; add salt. Cook until potatoes are just tender when pierced. Drain well and return to the pot over very low heat to dry out, about 3 minutes.

2. Mash the potatoes through a potato ricer or with an electric mixer, add the 2 egg yolks, milk, butter, pepper and nutmeg. Taste for salt.

3. Chop the tomatoes and put into a bowl. Season with salt and pepper, add the crum-bled feta cheese, olives and olive oil.

4. Preheat the broiler.

5. Put the potatoes into a piping bag with a large star tip. Pipe 12 potato nests starting with a base and then building the sides 1 inch high. Whisk together the egg yolk and the water. With a very soft pastry brush, brush the nests with the egg wash. Put under the broiler to lightly brown. Fill each nest with the tomato mixture and put back into the oven on a low shelf to heat the filling through. Garnish with parsley.

[SERVES 6, 2 NESTS PER PERSON]

A classic French potato dish, Potatoes Anna is very satisfying and versatile.

Potatoes Anna

3 pounds baking potatoes
2 teaspoons kosher salt
½ teaspoon white pepper

¼ cup unsalted butter (if using salted butter, use 1½ teaspoons kosher salt)

4 tablespoons chopped parsley, saving 1 tablespoon for garnish (or substitute 2 tablespoons chopped rosemary or mint)

1. Preheat the oven to 450 degrees F.

2. Peel the potatoes and then slice 1/8 inch thick or less on a mandolin or with a food processor slicing blade. Dry well on paper towels. Combine the salt and pepper in a small bowl.

3. In a 10-inch ovenproof nonstick pan with about 2-inch sides, melt the butter over medium heat. Swirl the butter around the pan to coat and then pour the rest into a bowl or measuring cup. Arrange the potatoes in a decorative, circular pattern overlapping the slices, completely covering the bottom of the pan. Brush with some of the melted butter. Season with a pinch of the salt and pepper and sprinkle with a little of the parsley. Arrange the rest of the potatoes (patted dry on paper towels) in non-composed layers,

brushed with butter, sprinkled with salt and parsley until you use all the potatoes. Drizzle with any remaining butter, top with a flat plate and press down with your hand to press the potatoes together. Remove the plate and cover the potatoes. On the top of the stove, cook the potatoes over medium heat until the bottom layer has browned lightly.

4. Place the potatoes in the middle of the oven and cook for 15 minutes. Take the cover off and cook 20 minutes more, or until they are cooked through.

5. Loosen the edges of the potatoes with a spatula, place a large serving platter over the top of the pan and invert the potatoes onto the platter. Sprinkle with reserved parsley and slice into wedges to serve.

[SERVES 8]

Red Bean–Pineapple Rice

½ cup long-grain rice	2 green onions, finely chopped	1 cup chopped fresh pineapple
½ teaspoon salt	1 red bell pepper, finely chopped	1 cup canned small red beans, drained
1 tablespoon olive oil	2 tomatoes, skinned, seeded and finely chopped	Salt and pepper to taste

1. Put the rice into a small saucepan, add the salt and cover with cold water about 1/2 inch over the top of the rice. Bring to a boil, cover and lower to the lowest setting. Cook until all the liquid has evaporated, about 10 minutes.

2. In a medium pan, over medium heat, heat the olive oil and sauté the green onions and bell peppers until wilted, about 3 minutes. Add the tomatoes, pineapple, beans and cooked rice. Season with salt and pepper. Cook until heated through.

VARIATION: Use mango instead of the pineapple. You can also change the flavor by adding 1/4 teaspoon toasted and ground cumin seeds with the bell pepper and stirring in 1/4 cup chopped cilantro just before serving.

[SERVES 6]

Orzo is a rice-shaped pasta that is very popular in Greece. It is available in most grocery stores and in Middle Eastern stores. Cook it in a large pot of boiling water the same way you would any other dried pasta.

Sonoran-Flavored Orzo Pasta

1 poblano chile, roasted and peeled
2 tablespoons vegetable oil
1 white onion, chopped
1 clove garlic, crushed

1 red bell pepper, cored and diced
1 cup corn
1 cup canned black beans, drained and rinsed
1 teaspoon salt

2 cups orzo pasta
Zest of 1 lime
Juice of 1 lime
1 cup grated Parmesan cheese
1 cup chopped cilantro
Salt and pepper to taste

1. Roast the chile under the broiler or over a flame until quite charred. Put it into a plastic bag to sweat for 10 minutes. The skin will come off easily with the help of a small knife. Cut the stem off the chile and cut out the ribs and seeds; discard and then finely chop the chile.

2. In a medium skillet, over medium heat, add the oil and the onion. Cook until the onion has wilted, about 10 minutes. Add the garlic and cook for 1 minute more. Add the bell pep-per and chile and cook for 5 minutes, and then add the corn and black beans to heat through.

3. Bring a large pot of water to a boil and add salt and orzo pasta. Cook the orzo until it is only just soft, about 7 minutes. Drain well and put into a bowl. Toss in the vegetable mixture, lime zest and juice, Parmesan cheese and cilantro. Taste for salt and pepper. Can be served hot or room temperature.

[SERVES 8]

Summer Vegetable Ravioli

2 small Japanese eggplant (or ½ a regular eggplant), diced
2 medium zucchini, diced
1 teaspoon salt
6 tablespoons olive oil, divided
1 small red onion, finely chopped
1 red bell pepper, seeded and chopped
1 serrano chile, seeded and fine-ly chopped
2 tomatoes, peeled, seeded and finely chopped
2 tablespoons chopped cilantro
Salt and pepper to taste
1 package round wonton wrappers

SAUCE
½ cup coconut cream
½ cup Vegetable Stock (page 74)
¼ cup dry sherry or Chinese rice wine
1 tomato, peeled, seeded and very finely chopped
½ teaspoon sambal oelek chile sauce
2 tablespoons oyster sauce
2 teaspoons cornstarch

1. Put the eggplant and zucchini into a sieve and sprinkle with the salt. Allow the vegetables to drain for 20 minutes. Pat dry with a paper towel.

2. Preheat the oven to 400 degrees F.

3. Toss the eggplant and zucchini in 4 table-spoons olive oil, put onto an oiled baking sheet and bake, stirring every now and then until the vegetables begin to brown, about 15 to 20 minutes.

4. In a medium frying pan over medium-high heat, heat the remaining olive oil. Sauté the onion until it has softened, and then add the bell pepper and chile; cook until softened, about 5 minutes. Stir in the tomatoes and cilantro and cook until the mixture is dry. Stir in the cooked eggplant and zucchini. Taste for salt and pepper. Allow to cool. This filling can be made up to 2 days in advance.

5. Fill one round wonton wrapper with a small spoonful of the vegetable mixture. Dampen the edges with a little water and top with a second wrapper. Seal the edges. Bring a large pot of water to a boil. Add 1 tea-spoon salt. Cook the ravioli a few at a time. When they float to the top, they are done cooking. Put onto an oiled pan in a single layer until serving time. Place 4 on a plate and drizzle with the sauce.

SAUCE

6. Mix all the ingredients together, put into a saucepan and bring to a boil. If it seems too thick, add a little of the cooking water.

VARIATION: Leftover filling can be used in a frittata or omelet, or piled onto a slice of French bread that has been brushed with olive oil and toasted and then served as an appetiz-er.

[SERVES 6]

Reading a Recipe and Measuring

1

1. Staff member Cynthia answers a recipe question.

2. A group effort on recipe interpretation.

3. Using the right measuring technique is important.

4. Just the right amount of lime juice!

This is the easiest way to cook vegetables. Try to cut them all the same size so they cook evenly. If using red beets, do not stir the mixture too much or everything will turn red with beet juice. Red beets and carrots add sweetness.

Roasted Vegetables

1 red yam, peeled
4 carrots, peeled
2 parsnips, peeled

4 medium Yukon Gold potatoes, scrubbed
6 shallots, skinned
¼ cup olive oil

1 teaspoon salt
Few grinds of pepper
2 tablespoons balsamic vinegar

1. Preheat the oven to 425 degrees F or 400 degrees F on convection roast setting.
2. Cut all the vegetables in pieces the same size as the shallots. Place in a bowl and toss with the olive oil, salt and pepper. Pour the vegetables into a roasting pan or baking sheet and bake for 40 to 45 minutes or until soft and brown. Stir them once or twice during cook-ing. Sprinkle with the balsamic vinegar before serving.

VARIATION: Grate some Parmesan cheese over the top while still hot. You can also use red onion, fennel bulb, peeled red beets, rutabagas and turnips.

[SERVES 6]

The addition of chiles to this dish adds a little heat. These can
be omitted if you would like a more mild-flavored dish. Do not allow this
dish to stand uncooked as the potatoes turn gray.

Potato and Leek Gratin

1   cup leeks (1 medium-sized
    leek)
2   tablespoons butter
2   cloves garlic, minced
1   tablespoon butter

2   tablespoons flour
1¾ cups Chicken Stock (page 72)
1   cup milk (any kind)
6   medium baking potatoes
1   (8-ounce) can chopped green

    chiles
1   cup grated sharp cheddar
    cheese
½   cup grated Romano cheese
2   teaspoons salt, divided

1. Preheat oven to 375 degrees F.
2. Cut off any green from the leeks, slice in
half lengthwise and rinse well. Slice the leek
into thin slices. In a medium skillet, over
medium-high heat, melt the butter. Add the
leeks and cook for about 5 minutes; do not
brown. Add the garlic and cook for an additional minute; set aside.
3. Melt the 1 tablespoon butter over low heat
in a saucepan, add flour, cook and stir for 2 to
3 minutes. Slowly stir in the stock and milk,
simmer and whisk the sauce until smooth and
slightly thickened.
4. Butter a shallow 3-quart baking dish. Peel
the potatoes and cut into 1/8-inch slices (use

a mandolin or slicing blade of a food processor). Arrange half the potatoes in prepared
baking dish. Top with half the leek and garlic
mixture and half the green chiles. Top with
half of the cheddar and Romano cheeses and
1 teaspoon salt. Repeat with the remaining
ingredients. Pour the broth/milk mixture over
the potatoes. Bake, uncovered, for 1 hour or
until browned and tender. Allow to stand for 5
minutes before serving.

[SERVES 8 TO 10]

Potatoes are a starch that requires a reasonable amount of salt. The olives will add some, but taste to make sure the dish is properly seasoned.

Provençal Mashed Potatoes

3 pounds baking potatoes
1 teaspoon salt
1 cup milk
2 tablespoons olive oil

¼ cup unsalted butter
2 large cloves garlic
4 ounces goat cheese
3 plum tomatoes, seeded and diced

16 black kalamata olives, pitted and chopped
¼ teaspoon white pepper
1 tablespoon chopped chives
Salt to taste

1. Peel the potatoes and cut into 2-inch pieces. Put the potatoes into a pot with the salt and cover with cold water. Bring to a boil, lower the heat and cook for about 15 minutes, or until tender. Drain and force through a potato ricer or mash with a masher.

2. While the potatoes are cooking, in a small pot bring the milk, olive oil, butter and garlic to a boil. Stir in the goat cheese to melt. Add to the potatoes and mix well. Add the diced tomatoes, olives, pepper and chives. Taste for salt.

[SERVES 8]

This dish is like a fall vegetable stew. The addition of the couscous turns it into a complete starch and vegetable side dish.

Vegetable Couscous

¼ cup olive oil

1 leek, cut in half, washed well and thinly sliced

1 small white onion, thinly sliced

3 cloves garlic, crushed

2 cups Chicken Stock (page 72)

1 cup butternut squash, peeled and cut into ½-inch dice

1 small carrot, peeled and cut into ½-inch dice

1 medium zucchini, cut into 1½-inch dice

1 medium yellow crookneck squash, cut into ½-inch dice

½ cup frozen baby lima beans

½ cup canned garbanzo beans, drained and rinsed

1 small serrano chile, seeded and chopped

1 teaspoon turmeric

½ teaspoon ground ginger

¼ teaspoon ground cinnamon

1 teaspoon salt

½ teaspoon freshly ground pepper

3 plum tomatoes, skinned, seeded and diced

½ cup frozen peas, defrosted

1 cup couscous

½ cup chopped cilantro leaves

1. In a large pot, heat the olive oil. Add the leek and onion, cover and allow to cook over medium-low heat for about 3 minutes. Uncover and add the garlic. Cook for 1 minute. Add the Chicken Stock, squash, carrot, zucchini, yellow squash, lima and garbanzo beans, chile, turmeric, ginger, cinnamon, salt and pepper. Increase the heat and bring to a boil. Cover and cook until the vegetables are just tender, about 5 minutes after the mixture comes to a boil. Take off the heat, stir in the tomatoes, peas and couscous. Cover and allow to stand for 10 minutes. Turn out onto a serving platter and sprinkle with the cilantro.

[SERVES 8]

This is a fragrant rice dish that pairs well with southwestern flavors.

Cinnamon Rice with Pine Nuts

- 2 tablespoons butter
- ½ cup finely chopped peeled carrots
- ½ cup finely chopped celery
- ½ cup finely diced white onion
- 2 cups long-grain rice
- 1 teaspoon salt
- 1 tablespoon ground cinnamon
- 4 cups Vegetable Stock (page 74) or water
- ½ cup dried currants
- ½ cup pine nuts, toasted in a dry frying pan

1. In a large saucepan over medium heat, melt the butter. Add the carrots, celery and onion. Cover the pan and cook for 10 minutes, stirring occasionally. Add the rice, salt, cinnamon, stock and currants. Raise the heat and bring to a boil. Cover and turn the heat to low; simmer for 20 minutes, stirring occasionally. Fold the toasted pine nuts into the rice.

[SERVES 8]

Creamy Polenta

- 4 cups Chicken or Vegetable Stock (see pages 72 and 74)
- 1 cup polenta (fine cornmeal)
- ¼ cup cream
- ¾ cup grated Parmesan cheese
- 2 tablespoons butter
- salt and pepper to taste

1. In a large saucepan, combine the stock and polenta. Stirring constantly, bring to a boil and cook until thickened, about 5 minutes after coming to a boil. Stir in the cream, cheese and butter. Taste for salt and pepper. This needs to be made very close to serving time to keep it smooth and creamy.

[SERVES 6]

Polenta was a staple and many times the only food available during World War II in Italy. It has enjoyed a revival and can be served in a creamy version like this or with less liquid poured into a pan and cut into serving-size pieces.

Couscous is a granular semolina served with most dishes in North Africa. We use instant couscous in our recipes—it just needs to be rehydrated with boiling liquid.

Couscous with Mint, Toasted Almonds and Lemon

3 tablespoons butter, divided
½ cup slivered almonds
1¾ cups Vegetable Stock (page 74)
½ teaspoon salt
1¼ cups couscous
Few grinds of fresh pepper
¼ cup chopped mint
Zest of 1 lemon

1. In a small frying pan, melt 1 tablespoon butter and add the almonds. Cook over medium heat until the almonds become lightly browned; set aside.

2. In a medium saucepan, bring the stock, 2 tablespoons butter and the salt to a boil. Remove from the heat and add the couscous. Allow to stand for 5 minutes. With a fork fluff the couscous, taste for salt, add the pepper and fold in the mint, lemon zest and almonds. Transfer to a serving bowl. This dish can be quickly put together at the last minute or made ahead and reheated in the microwave.

[SERVES 6]

Saffron-Scented Rice

1 teaspoon saffron, loosely packed
½ teaspoon sugar
2 tablespoons boiling water
1½ cups basmati rice
1 teaspoon salt
4 cardamom pods
2 sticks cinnamon
2¼ cups water

1. Crush the saffron in a mortar and pestle with the sugar. Add the boiling water and allow to steep. Wash the rice well and drain. In a large pot with a tight fitting lid, combine the rice, salt, cardamom, cinnamon and water. Bring to a boil. Add the saffron mixture, cover, lower the heat to simmer and cook about 20 minutes. Remove the cardamom and cinnamon sticks. Taste for salt. Cover and cook for 5 to 10 minutes more, or until the rice is cooked through.

[SERVES 6]

When using saffron, make sure it is the deep red variety. If you cannot find saffron, a good substitute would be 1/2 teaspoon turmeric plus 1/2 teaspoon mild paprika. The flavor will be different but the color will be lovely. You can also use any long-grain rice in place of the basmati rice.

Risotto is made with Arborio rice, a fat ivory
grain that releases a creamy starch when cooked.

Lemon Risotto with Basil

6 cups Chicken Stock (page 72)
2 tablespoons unsalted butter
1 medium red onion, finely
   chopped
1 celery rib, finely chopped, plus
   ¼ cup chopped leaves

½ serrano chile, minced
Salt and freshly ground pepper
1 clove garlic, minced
1½ cups Arborio rice
½ cup white vermouth
½ cup freshly grated Parmesan
   cheese

⅓ cup mascarpone cheese
1½ tablespoons finely grated
   lemon zest
2 tablespoons fresh lemon juice
¼ cup chopped basil leaves, plus
   2 tablespoons for garnish

1. Bring the stock to a boil in a medium saucepan, cover and keep hot. Melt the butter in a large wide saucepan. Add the onion, celery and chile. Season with salt and pepper and cook over low heat, stirring until softened, about 5 minutes. Add the garlic and cook for 2 minutes. Stir in the rice. Add the vermouth and simmer over moderate heat until almost absorbed, about 3 minutes. Add the hot stock, 1 cup at a time, stirring constantly between additions, until it is mostly absorbed before adding another cupful. The rice is done when it is tender and most of the liquid is absorbed, about 30 minutes total. Remove from the heat. Stir in 1/2 cup Parmesan cheese, mascarpone cheese, lemon zest and juice and 1/4 cup chopped basil. Season to taste with salt and pepper. Garnish with more basil.

[SERVES 6]

You can use any mixture of potatoes that you have on hand for this dish.

Mixed Potato Gratin

ROASTED GARLIC PUREE

1 head garlic
1 tablespoon olive oil

POTATO GRATIN

¼ cup unsalted butter
1 large russet potato, peeled and thinly sliced

2 large Yukon gold potatoes, peeled and thinly sliced
1 medium red yam, peeled and thinly sliced
1 medium sweet potato, peeled and thinly sliced
1½ teaspoons salt
¼ teaspoon white pepper
Pinch of fresh nutmeg

1 tablespoon chopped fresh oregano
1 tablespoon chopped fresh rosemary
1 cup whipping cream
1 cup milk

ROASTED GARLIC PUREE

1. Preheat the oven to 350 degrees F.
2. Slice off the top 1/4 inch from the garlic bulb. Use a garlic baker or wrap the garlic in foil after drizzling it with olive oil. Bake for 30 minutes until the garlic is a caramel color. Cool and squeeze the garlic out of its skin. Mash with a fork.

POTATO GRATIN

3. Preheat the oven to 400 degrees F. Grease a 9 x 13 x 2-inch baking pan with the butter. Layer the sliced potatoes in the baking pan.

4. In a small saucepan mix together the salt, pepper, nutmeg, oregano, rosemary, cream, milk and 1 tablespoon Roasted Garlic Puree. Bring to a boil and pour over the potatoes. Bake for 30 minutes, or until the potatoes are bubbly and browned on top. Check with a sharp knife or skewer to see if the potatoes are cooked all the way through. Allow to sit for 10 minutes before serving.

[SERVES 8]

Vegetables

It is open season for most vegetables these days. Today, if it is fresh any-
where in the world it is most often available in our markets. I like to
steam my vegetables and have a stackable steamer so I can put them on
to cook at different times. If I am cooking for company I steam or parboil
my green vegetables earlier in the day, plunge them into iced water to
chill them down and stop the cooking process, then pat them dry with a
paper towel. Doing this also enhances the bright green color. Heat the
vegetables in the microwave before serving.

Culinary Skills

In many recipes I have said you need to peel the tomato, roast or cut up a chile or pepper. So I did not have to repeat explaining these skills I have referred you to this page of explanations. These are culinary skills that make cooking easier.

To peel a tomato or a peach: Bring a pot of water to a boil. Cut an X in the non-stem end of the tomato and then gently lower into the boiling water for 30 seconds. Lift tomato out of the water and allow to cool until you can handle it. The skin should easily peel off starting where the X was made. To remove the seeds, cut the tomato into quarters and remove the seeds with your thumb or a teaspoon.

To roast a bell pepper: Cut the pepper in half and remove the seeds and the white ribs. Put small slits in each end so that the pepper lays flat on a baking sheet. Place under a hot broiler until the skin is black and charred. Transfer to a plastic bag to sweat for about 10 minutes. Using a small knife, peel off the skin.

To chop a small chile: Chiles have an oil that adheres to your fingers and is very painful if you get it in your eyes. Chopping a chile this way minimizes contact. Using a very sharp knife, cut the tip off the chile to create a flat surface so the chile stands up. Hold onto the stem and put the trimmed end on a cutting board. Carefully slice from the stem end to the tip cutting all the flesh off the chile. You should end up with the stem, white ribs, and seeds all attached. Discard this and chop the chile flesh.

To shuck corn: Using a Bundt pan, stand the stalk of the corn upright in the center hole of the pan. Using a sharp knife, cut the corn off the cob—it will fall into the main part of the pan and not be all over your counter.

Using a piping bag: Place the bag between your thumb and first finger. Fold the top half of the bag back over your hand and fill the bottom part of the bag. This prevents the top of the bag from getting messy. Place the filled bag in your right hand between the thumb and first finger, twist the top of the bag over the filling until it begins to come out the tip. Squeeze with your right hand and gently direct the piping bag with your left hand.

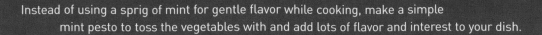

Instead of using a sprig of mint for gentle flavor while cooking, make a simple
mint pesto to toss the vegetables with and add lots of flavor and interest to your dish.

Petite Beans and Peas with Mint Pesto

MINT PESTO
1 cup tightly packed mint leaves
1 clove garlic
½ cup pine nuts, toasted
½ cup olive oil
¼ cup grated Parmesan cheese

BEANS AND PEAS
¼ cup pine nuts
1 pound petite green beans, stemmed
½ pound fresh snow peas, stemmed

1 (14-ounce) package frozen baby lima beans, defrosted
2 cups petite frozen peas, defrosted

MINT PESTO

1. Combine all the ingredients in a food processor or blender and puree. Taste for salt and pepper.
2. Dry toast the pine nuts in a small frying pan over medium heat; stir gently and be careful not to burn them.
3. Bring a large pot of water to a boil. Add the green beans and cook until still slightly crispy. Scoop the beans out of the boiling water and put into the bowl of cold water to chill down (this preserves the color). Repeat the process with the snow peas and boil for about 1 minute. When cooled, take the beans and snow peas out of the water and drain on a paper towel and pat dry.
4. Put all the beans and peas into a microwave-safe container, toss with as much pesto as needed. Just before serving, reheat in the microwave on high for about 1 1/2 minutes; sprinkle with the toasted pine nuts and serve. This is a great side dish for lamb.

VARIATION: Substitute almonds for the pine nuts.

[SERVES 8 TO 10]

Green Beans with Cherry Tomatoes

1 pound green beans, ends trimmed

1 cup cherry tomatoes, cut in half
1 tablespoon roasted garlic oil

1 teaspoon balsamic vinegar
Salt and pepper

1. Bring a large pot of water to a boil. Add the beans and cook until just tender. Strain and put the beans into a bowl of iced water until they are cold. This stabilizes the green color. Remove the beans from the ice bath. and drain well on a paper towel. Toss with the tomatoes, garlic oil, vinegar and salt and pepper. This can be done 3 to 4 hours in advance and then reheat in the microwave before serving.

HINT: If you cannot find roasted garlic oil, roast 2 cloves of garlic wrapped in foil until caramelized; cool and mash and then add to 1 cup extra virgin olive oil. Keep in the refrigerator.

[SERVES 6]

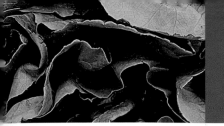

This dish goes well over soft polenta and can be used as a vegetarian alternative.

Sautéed Mushrooms with Spinach

2 tablespoons olive oil
1 medium red onion, thinly sliced
1 small clove garlic, crushed

½ pound button mushrooms, sliced
½ cup Vegetable or Chicken Stock (see pages 74 and 72)

1 pound fresh baby spinach, well washed
1 teaspoon balsamic vinegar
Salt and pepper to taste

1. In a large sauté pan over medium heat, heat the oil and cook the onion just until wilted. Add the garlic and cook for a few seconds. Add the mushrooms and cook until their juices have evaporated. Pour in the stock and raise the heat to bring to a boil. Toss in the spinach, vinegar, salt and pepper. Cook for a few seconds until the spinach has just wilted. Serve immediately.

[SERVES 6]

Zucchini Provençal

1 tablespoon olive oil
1 sweet onion, sliced
2 cloves garlic, crushed
1 pound zucchini, thinly sliced in circles

3 large tomatoes, peeled and finely chopped
¼ cup pitted, chopped black olives (preferably niçoise)
¼ teaspoon crushed red pepper

Salt and pepper to taste
2 tablespoons chopped Italian parsley

1. In a medium sauté pan, over medium-high heat, heat the olive oil. Add the onion and sauté until softened, about 5 minutes. Add the garlic and cook for a few seconds. Stir in the zucchini and cook until just softened, about 3 minutes. Add the tomatoes, olives and red pepper; season with salt and pepper. Cook until heated through. Transfer to a serving bowl and sprinkle with parsley.

[SERVES 6]

A good dish to use as a vegetarian sauce for pasta or over creamy polenta. If you have a mandolin, this is a quick way to slice the zucchini.

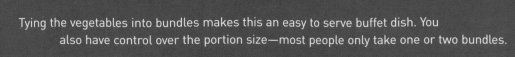
Tying the vegetables into bundles makes this an easy to serve buffet dish. You also have control over the portion size—most people only take one or two bundles.

Green Bean and Carrot Bundles

2   bunches green onions
1   pound green beans, preferably small thin ones

2   medium carrots
2   tablespoons butter

Salt and pepper
2   tablespoons chopped parsley

1.   Bring a medium-sized pot of water to a boil. Trim the green leaves off the onions and blanch the leaves in the boiling water for 1 minute. Cool in a bowl of iced water.

2.   Cut the ends off the beans, if they are long beans cut into about 3-inch lengths. Peel the carrots and cut into julienne pieces the same size as the beans. Stack the beans and car-rots together in 12 bundles and carefully tie together with the green onion strings. Place the bundles in a steamer and steam until ten-der, about 15 minutes. Carefully remove from the pot to a serving plate. Melt the butter and drizzle over the beans. Season with salt and pepper. Sprinkle with the parsley.

[SERVES 6]

Poultry

These tantalizing and easy to put together main dishes use chicken, game hens and turkey. When working with poultry, be very conscious of cleanliness—your hands, cutting board and your knife. I like to keep a bowl of warm soapy water with about 1 tablespoon of bleach in it in my sink to rinse hands and equipment. In the school and at home I use cotton shop towels for all my cleaning and then they go right into the washing machine. If the smell of raw poultry on your hand bothers you, wear gloves when you work. Just remember not to touch anything else until you have cleaned everything that has come in contact with the raw poultry.

A quick and easy pasta sauce that will please both the family and company.

Chicken and Shrimp Pasta Sauce

2 pounds chicken breasts
Salt and pepper
3 tablespoons olive oil
2 pounds fresh, ripe tomatoes, peeled, seeded and coarsely chopped

½ cup dry white wine
½ cup Chicken Stock (page 72)
2 cloves garlic, mashed
½ pound brown button mushrooms
2 tablespoons butter

½ pound frozen pearl onions
½ pound peeled large shrimp
2 tablespoons lemon juice
¼ cup chopped parsley
½ cup sliced fresh basil

Menu suggestions

Pear, Endive and
Stilton Salad
(page 89)

Buttermilk Panna Cotta
with Raspberry Sauce
(pages 209, 226)

Wine suggestions

Sauvignon Blanc

1. With a sharp knife, remove the white tendon from the chicken breast tender. Cut each chicken breast into 6 pieces. Dry on a paper towel and sprinkle with salt and pepper. In a large frying pan, heat the olive oil. When it is hot, brown the chicken pieces on all sides for about 5 minutes. Remove the breast meat from the pan and set aside.

2. Add the tomatoes to the frying pan with the white wine and stock. Add the garlic, cover and simmer for 30 minutes.

3. Wipe the mushrooms with a damp cloth and cut them in half. In a medium frying pan, add butter and heat until it sizzles. Add the mushrooms and the onions and cook until browned, about 10 minutes.

4. Add the shrimp to the sauce and simmer for about 3 minutes or until they turn pink. Return the chicken and any juices to the sauce, plus add the lemon juice, parsley, mushrooms and onions. Taste for salt and pepper. Serve garnished with the basil over fettuccini, linguini or angel hair pasta.

[SERVES 6]

This is an updated version of a classic French dish. If you cannot find
fresh tarragon, substitute 1 1/2 teaspoons dried for the 6 teaspoons fresh.

Chicken Cutlets Veronique

CHICKEN
6 boneless, skinless chicken
  breasts
6 teaspoons fresh tarragon,
  leaves only, chopped and divided
Salt and pepper

¼ cup unsalted butter

SAUCE
1 tablespoon butter
2 shallots, chopped
2 teaspoons chopped fresh tarragon leaves or ½ teaspoon dried

1 clove garlic, chopped
1½ cups seedless green or red
  grapes
1 cup dry white wine
1 cup whipping cream
Salt and pepper

Menu suggestions

French Onion Soup
(page 64)

Pommes Anna
(page 118)

Green Beans with
Cherry Tomatoes
(page 141)

Banana-White Chocolate
Bread Pudding,
or Apple Strudel
(pages 202, 230)

Wine suggestions

Chardonnay

1.   Remove the white tendon from the chick-
en breast by holding onto it and pulling while
you run a small paring knife along the tendon.
Place the breasts between two sheets of plastic wrap and pound to a 1/2-inch thickness.
Peel off the plastic and sprinkle each breast
with 1 teaspoon tarragon and a little salt and
pepper. In a sauté pan over medium-high
heat, melt half the butter. When hot, add 2
chicken breasts to the pan and sauté until
browned, about 4 minutes on each side.
Transfer to a plate. Repeat with the remaining
chicken breasts.

SAUCE
2. In the same unwashed sauté pan, melt
butter and add the shallots and tarragon.
Sauté over medium heat until the shallots
begin to soften, about 2 minutes. Add the garlic and cook for 1 minute. Add the grapes,
wine and cream. Boil until the sauce thickens
enough to coat a spoon. Taste for salt and
pepper. Put the chicken and any juices back
into the pan to heat through. To serve, spoon
the sauce over the chicken.

[SERVES 6]

Game hens are not as difficult to eat if you remove the backbone before cooking. Allow half a game hen per person. These are braised in a fragrant fruit sauce.

Braised Game Hens with Fruit and Honey

3 game hens
¾ cup flour
4 to 6 tablespoons olive oil, divided
2 medium onions, thinly sliced
1½ cups Chicken Stock (page 72)
½ cup finely chopped parsley

2 tablespoons skinned and grated fresh ginger
1 teaspoon cinnamon
½ teaspoon ground nutmeg
⅛ teaspoon ground cloves
½ cup honey

1 cup mixed dried fruit, very roughly chopped
⅓ cup golden raisins
½ cup slivered almonds
Chopped parsley to garnish

Menu suggestions

Baby Greens with Pomegranate Seeds and Spiced Pecans
(page 88)

Creamy Polenta
(page 134)

Green Beans with Cherry Tomatoes
(page 141)

Apple Strudel
(page 202)

Wine suggestions

Gewurztraminer

1. Cut the game hens through the breastbone to open up flat and then cut along each side of the backbone and remove. Trim away any fat. Dry with a paper towel and sprinkle each piece with 2 tablespoons flour.
2. Preheat the oven to 375 degrees F.
3. In a frying pan, heat 2 tablespoons olive oil. Two pieces at a time, brown the game hens on both sides. Transfer to a casserole large enough to hold six half hens. Continue browning the remaining hens. Add a little more oil to the frying pan and add the onions. Sauté until lightly browned, about 10 minutes. Add the stock, parsley, ginger, cinnamon, nutmeg and cloves. Bring to a boil, scraping any browned bits stuck to the bottom of the pan. This gives extra flavor to the sauce. Pour over the game hens, cover with a lid and place in the oven. Cook for 20 minutes. Add the honey, dried fruit and raisins to the sauce. Uncover and cook for 10 minutes more.
4. In a small frying pan, heat 2 tablespoons olive oil. Add the almonds and sauté until golden brown. Drain them on a paper towel.
5. To serve, put the game hen on a plate, spoon some of the sauce over it, sprinkle with the almonds and chopped parsley.

[SERVES 6]

This recipe works well in a soaked clay pot or a casserole. Quick, easy and with great flavor.

Chicken Wrapped in Prosciutto

6   fresh sage leaves
1   teaspoon fresh rosemary leaves
¾   teaspoon dried marjoram

¼   cup unsalted butter, melted
1   teaspoon salt
3   grinds fresh pepper

8   boneless, skinless chicken thighs
8   slices prosciutto
Chopped parsley to garnish

1. Preheat the oven to 400 degrees F.
2. Chop together the sage, rosemary and marjoram. Put into a bowl with the melted butter, salt and pepper.
3. Trim most of the fat off the chicken thighs, being careful not to cut them up. Separate the prosciutto slices. Dip the chicken thighs into the butter-herb mixture and then wrap in the prosciutto. Place in one layer in a casserole with a lid or a well soaked clay pot. Cover with the lid and cook for 20 minutes.
4. To serve, slice on the diagonal into 3 slices, drizzle with some of the cooking liquid and sprinkle with parsley.

[SERVES 4 TO 6]

Menu suggestions

Spinach Ravioli with
Chile-Tomato Cream
Sauce
(page 50)

Provençal
Mashed Potatoes
(page 131)

Green Beans with
Cherry Tomatoes
(page 141)

Strawberry Tiramisu
(page 204)

Wine suggestions

Pinot Gros or Pinot Grigio

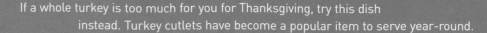

Herbed Turkey Cutlets with Cranberry Sauce

MARINADE
¼ cup chopped fresh thyme
Zest of 1 lemon
Juice of 1 lemon
½ cup chopped Italian parsley
1½ teaspoons salt
½ teaspoon freshly ground pepper

3 tablespoons olive oil
12 turkey breast cutlets

SAUCE
1 cup red wine
½ cup cranberry jelly
Sprig of thyme

1 small clove garlic, mashed
¼ cup dried cranberries
1 teaspoon cornstarch mixed
   with 1 tablespoon water
Salt and pepper
2 tablespoons chopped parsley
Creamy Polenta (page 134)

Menu suggestions

Spiced Butternut Squash
Soup with Stilton Biscuits
(pages 70, 197)

Sauteed Mushrooms
with Spinach
(page 144)

Pumpkin-Ginger
Cheesecake
(page 215)

Wine suggestions

Pinot Noir

MARINADE
1. Process all the marinade ingredients in a food processor or blender.

TURKEY
2. Put the turkey cutlets into a glass baking dish and cover with the marinade. Allow to marinate for 30 minutes or up to 2 hours.
3. To cook, grill under the broiler or in a grill pan greased with olive oil on top of the stove for 3 minutes on each side, or on a hot bar-beque for 2 minutes on each side. Serve as soon as they are cooked.

SAUCE
4. Bring the wine to a simmer in a small saucepan; add the cranberry jelly, thyme, garlic and dried cranberries and then simmer over low heat for 5 minutes. Take out the thyme and add the cornstarch mixture. Heat until the sauce thickens; season with salt and pepper and add the parsley.
5. To serve, place a cup of the polenta in the center of the plate, arrange two turkey cutlets on the polenta and spoon the cranberry sauce over top. Serve with a green salad or steamed green vegetables.

[SERVES 6]

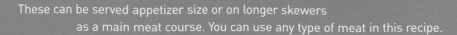

These can be served appetizer size or on longer skewers as a main meat course. You can use any type of meat in this recipe.

Turkey Satays with Peanut Sauce

2 pounds turkey breast, cut into 1-inch pieces

MARINADE
1 cup plain yogurt
¼ cup vegetable oil
1 tablespoon peeled and grated fresh ginger

½ teaspoon ground cardamom
½ teaspoon ground coriander
¼ teaspoon salt
¼ teaspoon white pepper
2 teaspoons paprika

PEANUT SAUCE
½ cup smooth peanut butter

1 cup boiling water
2 cloves garlic, minced
2 tablespoons fresh lemon juice
½ teaspoon crushed red pepper flakes
2 tablespoons molasses

Menu suggestions

Tropical Fruit Gazpacho
(page 74)

Red Bean and Pineapple Rice or Sonoran Flavored Orzo Pasta
(pages 122, 124)

Crêpes with Caramelized Bananas and Mexican Chocolate Ice Cream
(page 216)

Wine suggestions

Champagne or Sparkling Wine

1. Put the turkey cubes into a nonreactive dish. Mix the marinade ingredients together, pour over the turkey and stir. Cover and allow to marinate for 6 hours or overnight.
2. Preheat the barbecue grill to medium-high.
3. In a medium saucepan, combine all the sauce ingredients and whisk while it comes to a boil, then simmer for 2 to 3 minutes. Take off the heat and transfer to a serving bowl; set aside.
4. Thread the turkey onto 8 metal skewers or 16 bamboo skewers that have been soaked in water for 20 minutes. Barbecue for about 8 minutes, turning to make sure they are cooked all around. Serve with the Peanut Sauce.

[SERVES 8]

This is a very flavorful, festive dish using game hens.
You could also use chicken breasts, rack of lamb or pork tenderloin.

Mole-Rubbed Roast Game Hen with Tropical Fruit Salsa

MOLE RUB

1½ teaspoons chipotle chile powder

1½ tablespoons ancho chile powder

2 tablespoons kosher salt

1 tablespoon dried Mexican oregano, toasted in a small frying pan

1½ teaspoons cocoa powder

6 cloves garlic, crushed

2 tablespoons vegetable oil

⅓ cup fresh lime juice

3 game hens, cut in half along the breastbone, opened up and the backbone cut out making 6 halves

TROPICAL FRUIT SALSA

1 small red bell pepper, chopped finely

1 cup chopped ripe papaya

1 cup chopped ripe mango

1 habanero chile, seeded and chopped

1 tablespoon chopped cilantro

½ cup fresh orange juice

1 tablespoon lime juice

1 green onion, finely sliced

2 teaspoons chopped mint

1. For the mole, mix together the chile powders, salt, oregano, cocoa powder, crushed garlic, oil and lime juice in a small bowl. Using a pastry brush, brush the hen halves on both sides with the chile mixture. Refrigerate for at least 1 hour or overnight to marinate.

2. Heat the oven to 375 degrees F. Put the hens on a baking sheet and roast for 25 to 35 minutes, or until there is no redness in the thigh joint. Serve with the salsa.

3. Combine all the salsa ingredients. Use the same day as made.

[SERVES 6]

Menu suggestions

Gazpacho with Shellfish
(page 66)

Cinnamon Rice with Pine Nuts
(page 134)

Green Beans with Cherry Tomato
(page 141)

Praline Tacos or Chilled Mexican Chocolate Soufflé
(pages 226, 228)

Wine suggestions

Pinot Noir

This is a dish that has all the flavors of North Africa.

Saffron-Scented Chicken Breasts

1 cup Chicken Stock (page 72)
1 cup dried apricots
¼ cup pine nuts
1 teaspoon salt
½ teaspoon ground pepper
¼ teaspoon saffron threads

¼ teaspoon ground ginger
⅛ teaspoon ground cinnamon
1 teaspoon sugar
8 small boneless, skinless chicken breasts
2 tablespoons butter, divided

2 tablespoons olive oil, divided
1 onion, cut in half and thinly sliced

1. Bring the stock to a boil, take off the heat and add the apricots to soak. In a small dry frying pan, brown the pine nuts. With a mortar and pestle mix together the salt, pepper, saffron, ginger, cinnamon and sugar; finely grind.
2. One at a time, put the chicken breasts into a plastic bag and pound until they are an even thickness. If too large, cut in half. Dry the chicken on a paper towel.
3. In a 12-inch frying pan over medium-high heat, heat 1 tablespoon butter and 1 tablespoon oil. When hot, quickly brown 4 of the chicken breasts at a time, turning once. Remove from the pan to a platter. Sprinkle the chicken breasts with half the spice mixture. Repeat with the other 4 chicken breasts and sprinkle with the remaining spice mixture.

Add the remaining butter and oil to the pan. Sauté the onion until tender, about 5 minutes. Pour in the stock and apricots, and bring to a simmer. Add the chicken back to the pan, cover and cook over medium heat for about 7 to 10 minutes, or until the chicken is cooked through.
4. To serve, sprinkle with the pine nuts.

[SERVES 8]

Menu suggestions

Seafood Soup with
Garlic Aioli
(page 68)

Vegetable Couscous
or Couscous with Mint,
Toasted Almonds
and Lemon
(pages 132, 135)

Green Beans with
Cherry Tomatoes
(page 141)

Lemon Alaska
(page 205)

Wine suggestions

Reisling

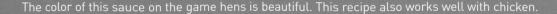

Roasted Game Hens with Spiced Raspberry Sauce

3 game hens

MARINADE
¼ cup dry vermouth
2 tablespoons oyster sauce
2 tablespoons olive oil
½ teaspoon pepper

SAUCE
¼ teaspoon cumin seeds
1 tablespoon vegetable oil
2 cloves garlic, crushed
2 tablespoons minced ginger
1 (12-ounce) package frozen
   raspberries, thawed
2 cups red wine
⅓ cup sugar
½ teaspoon Asian chile sauce

1 teaspoon salt
1 grind pepper
1 teaspoon cornstarch
1 tablespoon water
1 teaspoon balsamic vinegar

GARNISH
1 cup fresh raspberries
¼ cup chopped fresh chives

Menu suggestions

Avocados with
Shrimp Salad
(page 32)

Roasted Vegetables
(page 128)

Zucchini Provençal
(page 144)

Chocolate Mousse
in Orange Shells
(page 206)

Wine suggestions

Zinfandel

1. Cut the game hens along the breastbone and open up flat. Cut along each side of the backbone and remove. Combine the marinade ingredients and brush on each side of the game hens. Cover and allow to marinate 15 minutes or up to 4 hours.
2. For the sauce, put the cumin seeds in a small frying pan and toast over medium heat until very lightly brown. Put into a mortar and pestle and grind. In a medium-sized frying pan, heat the oil, add the garlic and ginger and cook for 1 minute over medium heat. Add the cumin, raspberries, wine, sugar, chile sauce, salt and pepper. Turn the heat to high and bring to a boil. Gently boil the mixture for about 20 minutes. Pour the sauce into a strainer and force the pulp through, scraping the underside of the strainer when finished.

Discard the seeds. Transfer sauce to a clean saucepan. In a separate bowl, mix the cornstarch with the water and then add to the sauce. Bring to a boil to thicken. Add the balsamic vinegar and keep warm.
3. Preheat the oven to 400 degrees F. Put the game hens skin side up onto an olive oil-greased baking sheet and put into the hot oven. Roast for 35 minutes. Bring out of the oven and allow to sit for 5 minutes before serving.
4. To serve, put one game hen on a plate, drizzle with the sauce and sprinkle with the raspberries and chopped chives.

HINT: To wash fresh raspberries without damaging them, sit them on a paper towel and spritz them with a water bottle. Allow them to air dry.

[SERVES 6]

These are best if they are cooked on a barbeque grill.
If you are unable to do that, use an indoor grill pan.

Spiced, Grilled Chicken Breasts with Avocado Salsa

8 boneless chicken breasts,
   preferably with skin on

MARINADE

2 teaspoons salt
1 teaspoon pepper
4 teaspoons ancho chile powder
1 tablespoon crushed garlic

1 teaspoon whole cumin, toasted
   and ground with a mortar and
   pestle
1 tablespoon Mexican oregano,
   toasted and crumbled
¼ teaspoon cinnamon
¼ teaspoon allspice
⅔ cup fresh lime juice
¼ cup vegetable oil

AVOCADO SALSA

3 avocados, peeled and chopped
3 plum tomatoes, chopped
¼ cup chopped white onion
1 jalapeno, seeded and chopped
¼ cup chopped cilantro (no
   stems)
3 tablespoons lime juice
Salt and pepper to taste

Menu suggestions

Avocado, Jicama
and Orange Salad
(page 78)

Sonoran-Flavored
Orzo Pasta
(page 124)

Chile-Corn Sticks
(page 194)

Chocolate Pecan Tart
with Caramel Sauce
(page 212)

Wine suggestions

Zinfandel

1. With a sharp knife, carefully remove the white tendon from the chicken breast. Combine the other ingredients and marinate the chicken breasts in a nonreactive pan for 30 minutes and no longer than 2 hours. Cook on a medium-hot grill or barbecue for 15 to 20 minutes, turning often. Serve with the salsa.

2. Mix all the salsa ingredients together in a nonreactive bowl. Make and serve in the same day.

[SERVES 8]

Canned chipotle chiles in adobo sauce are used in this recipe.
They are found in the Mexican section of the supermarket.

Sautéed Chicken with Chipotle-Orange Sauce

4 boneless, skinless chicken breasts

¾ cup buttermilk

1 cup panko (Japanese bread-crumbs)

Salt and pepper

2½ tablespoons unsalted butter, divided

1½ tablespoons vegetable oil

8 green onions, finely chopped

1 teaspoon chipotle chile in adobo sauce

2 tablespoons lemon juice

1 cup orange juice

2 tablespoons chopped cilantro

1. Between two pieces of plastic wrap, flatten the chicken with a pounder or the bottom of a saucepan until it is of even thickness. If the fillets are too big, cut them in half. Put the buttermilk into a bowl and the panko on a flat dish. Season the crumbs with salt and pepper. Dip the chicken breasts into the buttermilk and then into the panko.

2. Melt 1 1/2 tablespoons butter and the oil in a nonstick frying pan. When hot, sauté the chicken breasts 2 at a time, about 3 minutes on each side, until browned. Put onto a serving plate and keep warm. Repeat with the remaining chicken breasts.

3. To make the sauce, melt the remaining butter in the same sauté pan, add the green onions and cook for 1 minute. Add the chipotle chile, and lemon and orange juices. Bring to a boil, taste for salt and pepper. Boil until slightly thickened, about 3 minutes. Serve over the chicken breasts and garnish with the chopped cilantro.

[SERVES 6]

Menu suggestions

Sonoran Spinach Salad
(page 86)

Parmesan Crusted Potatoes
(page 116)

Green Beans with Cherry Tomatoes
(page 141)

Crêpes with Caramelized Bananas and Mexican Chocolate Ice Cream
(page 216)

Wine suggestions

Sauvignon Blanc or Fume Blanc

Meats

Roasting meats are the easiest way to cook. In fact, you can cook the entire meal in one oven. Pork is now considered "the other white meat" and comes in many delicious cuts that add great variety to your menus. Lamb is plentiful and very versatile, although to many it may be an acquired taste. For me, the aroma always stimulates memories of weekly family roast dinners. In Arizona the weather is so good that we can grill outside for most of the year. All recipes that use the barbecue can also be cooked indoors in a grill pan or roasted in the oven.

You can find dried hibiscus flowers in Middle Eastern and Mexican stores. Take the time to trim the lamb leg well; it is so much nicer to eat without the fat and gristle.

Barbecued Hibiscus-Marinated Lamb

4   cups cold water
4   large cloves garlic, smashed
1¼ cups dried hibiscus flowers
1   tablespoon salt
¼   cup sugar
1   (4- to 5-pound) boned leg of
    lamb
3   tablespoons olive oil

½   cup pomegranate seeds
Mint sprigs to garnish

SAUCE

1   cup reserved marinade
½   cup pomegranate jelly (or a
    whole 5-ounce jar)

¼   teaspoon red pepper flakes
2   teaspoons cornstarch or
    arrowroot
¼   cup water
Salt and pepper to season

Menu suggestions

Hot Goat Cheese Soufflé
with Arugula Salad
(page 38)

Couscous with Mint, Toasted
Almonds and Lemon
(page 135)

Petite Beans with Peas
and Mint Pesto
(page 140)

Chocolate Mousse in
Orange Shells
(page 206)

Wine suggestions

Zinfandel

1. In a medium saucepan, bring the water and garlic to a boil. Add the dried hibiscus and simmer for 5 minutes. Remove from the heat and add the salt and sugar. Allow to steep for 30 minutes. Strain the marinade to remove the blossoms and the garlic; chill.

2. Open the lamb leg and, with a small sharp knife, remove all the tendons, sinew and fat. It takes a while to do this, but is worth the time. Usually it is easier to cut the roast into 3 pieces where the bone was cut out. You can see where it naturally comes apart. Roll the roasts up, tucking any stray bits in and tie the meat together with cotton string into 3 small roasts. Put into a plastic bag and cover with the chilled marinade. Refrigerate, turning once or twice for 12 to 24 hours (it is best left 24 hours).

3. Heat the barbecue to high. When it reaches 450 degrees F, it is ready for the meat. Remove the meat from the marinade and pour the marinade into a small saucepan. Dry the meat on a paper towel and brush with the olive oil. Turn the grill down to medium low and barbecue for 10 to 15 minutes, turning the meat so it is browned on each side. Using an instant thermometer, check that the internal temperature of the meat registers 135 degrees F for medium-rare. Allow the meat to sit for 5 minutes before slicing into medallions. Garnish with the pomegranate seeds and mint. Serve with the sauce on the side.

4. For the sauce, bring the reserved marinade to a boil in a saucepan. Turn the heat to medium and add the pomegranate jelly and red pepper flakes. Stir until the jelly dissolves. Mix the cornstarch with the water and then add to the sauce. Bring to a simmer to thicken. Taste for salt and pepper.

[SERVES 8]

This is an updated version of a traditional British roast dinner. Prime meat is the best you can buy but is not always available. Choice meat is the most widely available.

Beef Rib Roast with Mustard-Thyme Crust and Herbed Yorkshire Puddings

2 large cloves garlic
2 teaspoons salt
2 tablespoons whole-grain Dijon mustard
1 tablespoon chopped fresh thyme
1 tablespoon olive oil

2 teaspoons ground pepper
2 tablespoons flour
1 (4- to 5-pound, 4 rib) beef rib roast

GRAVY
2 tablespoons fat from roasting pan
3 tablespoons flour

2 cups Beef or Vegetable Stock (pages 73 or 74), heated
Salt and pepper to taste

HORSERADISH CRÈME FRAÎCHE
¼ cup prepared horseradish
1 (8-ounce) container crème fraîche (or sour cream)

Menu suggestions

Roasted Red Pepper and Chile Soup
(page 75)

Mixed Potato Gratin or Roasted Vegetables
(pages 137, 128)

Green Bean and Carrot Bundles
(page 146)

Brandied Apple Mousse or Individual Frozen Lime Cheesecakes
(pages 219, 224)

Wine suggestions

Cabernet Sauvignon

1. With a mortar and pestle, mash the garlic with the salt. Mix in the mustard, thyme, oil and pepper.
2. Sprinkle the bottom of the roasting pan with flour and then place a roasting rack in the pan.
3. Trim most of the fat off the beef, but leave a little for flavor. Place fat side up on the roasting rack. Spread the top of the meat with the mustard mixture. Allow to sit at room temperature for 30 minutes.
4. Preheat the oven to 450 degrees F. Roast the beef for 15 minutes, lower the oven temperature to 375 degrees F and continue cooking until the internal temperature reaches 120 degrees F for rare or 130 degrees F for medium-rare (about 1 1/2 hours). Remove from the oven, cover the beef with foil and allow to rest

for 20 minutes before serving (this allows the meat to redistribute its juices). Serve with the gravy, Horseradish Crème Fraîche and Herbed Yorkshire Puddings.

GRAVY
5. Drain all but 2 tablespoons of fat from the roasting pan. Place the pan over medium heat and stir in the flour, scraping all the brown bits off the bottom of the pan. Cook for about 1 minute. Add the stock and bring to a boil. Taste for salt and pepper. If using canned stock, be careful of the salt. Serve in a gravy boat with the roast.

continued on page 172

¼ teaspoon salt
2 tablespoons chopped chives

HERBED YORKSHIRE PUDDING
4 large eggs
1 cup milk

½ cup water
2 cups flour
1 teaspoon salt
½ teaspoon white pepper
3 tablespoons chopped fresh
  chives

2 tablespoons chopped fresh
  thyme
3 tablespoons Crisco or vegetable
  oil

HORSERADISH CRÈME FRAÎCHE

6. Stir all the crème fraîche ingredients together. Can be made a day ahead.

HERBED YORKSHIRE PUDDING

7. Whisk together the eggs, milk and water in the bowl of an electric mixer. Sift in the flour, salt and pepper and mix well. Gently stir in the chives and thyme. Refrigerate for at least 1 hour or up to 8 hours. Stir well before using.

8. Preheat the oven to 450 degrees F.

9. Using a popover or muffin pan, (plus 4 ramekins), put about 1 teaspoon of Crisco or oil in each cup. Put into the oven and heat the oil until very hot, about 5 minutes. Using a soup ladle, carefully fill the 16 cups three-fourths full of the batter. Bake the pudding for 15 minutes, reduce the temperature to 350 degrees F and bake for another 20 minutes, or until the edges are brown and crisp. Remove from the pans and serve on a platter with the beef. The puddings will sink in the center. They are best right from the oven but can be made a few hours ahead and reheated in a 350-degree F oven on a baking sheet, until crisp, just before serving.

[SERVES 8]

This dish is wonderful hot or cold. You can also use a larger pork loin and cook it longer.

Braised Pork Tenderloin with Whiskey-Soaked Dried Plums

⅓ cup whiskey
18 dried plums (prunes)
2 pork tenderloins, about 2 ½
   pounds total
¼ cup Dijon mustard

½ cup dark brown sugar
2 tablespoons vegetable oil
1 cup Beef Stock (page 73)
¼ teaspoon salt
Few grinds of pepper
1 bay leaf

1 sprig fresh thyme
1 sprig parsley
2 teaspoons cornstarch
1 tablespoon water
Watercress to garnish

1. Gently heat the whiskey in a pot or in the microwave until warm. Put the dried plums in a bowl and pour the whisky over them. Allow to steep until ready to use.

2. Trim any silver skin from the tenderloins. Mix together the mustard and brown sugar and coat the tenderloins with the mixture.

3. In a frying pan with a lid, heat the vegetable oil over medium-high heat until hot. Add the pork tenderloins and brown on all sides. Pour in the stock, whiskey and plums, salt, pepper and fresh herbs. Cover the pan,

lower the heat to low and cook the meat for 10 to 15 minutes, or until the internal temperature reaches 140 degrees F. Take the meat and plums out of the pan and keep warm. Remove and discard the fresh herbs. Taste the sauce for salt and pepper. Mix the cornstarch with the water and add to the sauce. Bring to a boil to thicken.

4. Slice the meat on a platter, surround with the plums, garnish with the watercress and serve the sauce alongside.

[SERVES 6]

Menu suggestions

Arugula, Avocado
and Prosciutto Salad
(page 84)

Parmesan
Crusted Potatoes
(page 116)

Zucchini Provençal
(page 144)

Apple Strudel with
Whipped Cream
(page 202)

Wine suggestions

Merlot

This has a spicy marinade and is wonderful served with the Creamy Corn Sauce. When carving, slice across the meat grain and it will be very tender.

Spiced Flank Steak with Creamy Corn Sauce

MARINADE
¼ cup soy sauce
2 tablespoons sesame oil
2 cloves garlic, minced
1 tablespoon grated fresh ginger
Zest of 1 lemon
1 serrano chile, seeded and chopped
2 star anise pods, finely crushed

FLANK STEAK
1 pound flank steak
2 tablespoons chopped parsley to garnish

CREAMY CORN SAUCE
¼ cup water
2 teaspoons unsalted butter
2 small shallots, finely chopped

1 clove garlic, thinly sliced
2 large ears of corn, kernels cut off (as shown on page 142)
¾ cup Chicken Stock (page 72)
½ teaspoon salt
Pinch of ground white pepper
2 tablespoons heavy cream

Menu suggestions
Gazpacho with Shellfish
(page 66)

Sonoran-Flavored
Orzo Pasta
(page 124)

Crêpes with Caramelized
Bananas and Mexican
Chocolate Ice Cream
(page 216)

Wine suggestions
Zinfandel or Sangiovese

MARINADE

1. In a small bowl, combine all the marinade ingredients. Pour the marinade into a large zip-lock plastic bag. Add the flank steak, seal the bag and refrigerate for 6 to 12 hours, turning once or twice.

CREAMY CORN SAUCE

2. Combine the water, butter, shallots and garlic in a small saucepan and bring to a simmer. Cook over medium heat, stirring occasionally, until the shallots are translucent, about 3 minutes. Add the corn and stock and cook over medium heat until tender, about 7 minutes.

3. In batches, transfer to a blender or food processor and blend until smooth, about 2 minutes. Strain the sauce into a clean saucepan and season with salt and white pepper. Boil down until reasonably thick, about 5 minutes. Whisk in the cream just before serving.

FLANK STEAK

4. Light a grill or heat a cast-iron grill pan on the top of the stove until very hot. Remove the meat from the marinade and rinse under cold water; pat dry. Grill the flank steak over high heat, turning once, about 3 minutes on each side for medium-rare meat. Transfer the steak to a cutting board and let stand for 10 minutes.

5. Thinly slice the steak across the grain and arrange the slices on warmed plates. Drizzle with the Creamy Corn Sauce and garnish with chopped parsley.

[SERVES 4]

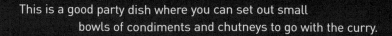
This is a good party dish where you can set out small bowls of condiments and chutneys to go with the curry.

Curried Lamb

4 tablespoons vegetable oil, divided
3 pounds boneless lamb, cut into ¾-inch pieces
3 tablespoons all-purpose flour
Salt and pepper
1 onion, finely chopped

3 cloves garlic, minced
1 tablespoon curry powder
1 teaspoon ground coriander
1 teaspoon ground cumin
½ teaspoon ground ginger
¼ teaspoon cayenne pepper
2 cups Beef Stock (page 73)

½ cup golden raisins
Zest of 1 lemon
Juice of 1 lemon
1 Granny Smith apple, peeled, cored and cut into small cubes
1 cup plain yogurt

Menu suggestions

Spiced Butternut Squash Soup
(page 70)

Avocado, Jicama and Orange Salad
(page 78)

Saffron-Scented Rice
(page 135)

Frozen Lemon Soufflé Cake
(page 221)

Wine suggestions

Try beer with this one!

1. In a medium frying pan, over medium-high heat, heat 2 tablespoons oil until hot. Dry the meat on a paper towel. Sprinkle with the flour, salt and pepper. Add a few pieces of meat at a time to the frying pan and brown on all sides. Transfer the meat to a plate. Add the remaining oil and sauté the onion until soft, about 3 minutes. Add the garlic, curry powder, coriander, cumin, ginger and cayenne pepper. Cook for 1 minute. Return the lamb and any juices to the pan and add the stock, raisins, lemon zest and juice. Cover, bring to a boil then turn the heat to a simmer and cook for 30 minutes. Add the cubed apple and simmer for another 30 minutes until the meat is tender. Stir in the yogurt and transfer lamb to a serving dish. Serve with the accompaniments in small dishes on the side. Some great sides dishes include saffron rice, roasted peanuts, toasted coconut, chopped pineapple and mango or mango chutney.

[SERVES 6]

I use racks of Australian lamb for this recipe.
You could use individual lamb chops and adjust the cooking time.

Lamb in an Herb Crust

1 tablespoon finely chopped
  fresh rosemary

2 tablespoons finely chopped
  parsley

½ teaspoon dried marjoram

½ cup dried breadcrumbs

½ teaspoon Chinese five-spice
  powder

Ground black pepper

2 racks of lamb chops, trimmed
  of most of the fat

½ teaspoon kosher salt

1 cup flour

3 egg whites, beaten until foamy

ORANGE AND HONEY SAUCE

1½ cups Beef Stock (page 73)

½ cup Madeira wine

1 sprig fresh rosemary

1 clove garlic

⅓ cup orange juice

1 tablespoon honey

Salt and pepper

2 teaspoons arrowroot or cornstarch

2 tablespoons water

Zest of ½ an orange

1. Mix the rosemary, parsley, marjoram, breadcrumbs, spice and pepper together in a flat dish. Season the lamb with the salt and then roll in the flour and shake off the excess. Dip in the beaten egg whites, and then roll in the breadcrumb mixture. Firmly pat the breadcrumb coating into place. Cover and refrigerate until ready to cook. Make the sauce.

2. For the sauce, place the stock and wine in a pot with the rosemary and garlic. Bring to a boil, reduce heat and simmer for 20 minutes. Add the orange juice and honey. Season with

salt and pepper. Remove the rosemary and garlic from the stock. Thicken the sauce by adding the arrowroot mixed with the 2 table-spoons water and then bring it to a boil. Cover the sauce and set aside until time to serve.

3. When ready to serve, reheat the sauce and stir in the orange zest. Serve in a bowl along-side the lamb.

4. To cook the lamb, reheat the oven to 375 degrees F. Place lamb on a greased baking sheet and cook for 20 to 25 minutes, or until the lamb is cooked to 130 degrees F (using an instant thermometer). Allow to rest in a warm place for 5 minutes before slicing into serving pieces.

[SERVES 6]

Menu suggestions

Gazpacho with Shellfish
(page 66)

Provençal Potatoes
(page 131)

Sautéed Mushrooms
with Spinach
(page 144)

Hazelnut and
Raspberry Pavlova
(page 222)

Wine suggestions

Zinfandel

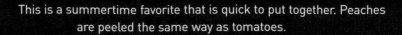

This is a summertime favorite that is quick to put together. Peaches are peeled the same way as tomatoes.

Rosemary-Grilled Lamb Chops with Peach-Mint Salsa

PEACH-MINT SALSA
4 ripe peaches, peeled and chopped (see peeling a peach on page 142)
½ red bell pepper, seeds and ribs removed, diced
1 tablespoon chopped red onion

1 serrano chile, seeds and ribs removed, diced finely
¼ cup fresh lime juice
2 teaspoons honey
½ teaspoon balsamic vinegar
4 tablespoons chopped fresh mint
½ teaspoon salt
3 grinds fresh pepper

LAMB CHOPS
16 lamb loin chops
2 tablespoons olive oil
1 teaspoon salt
2 tablespoons finely chopped rosemary leaves

Menu suggestions

Avocados with Shrimp Salad
(page 32)

Lemon Risotto with Basil
(page 136)

Frozen Lemon Soufflé Cake
(page 221)

Wine suggestions

Zinfandel

1. Combine all the salsa ingredients in a nonmetallic bowl. Refrigerate for 30 minutes before serving for the flavors to blend.
2. Brush the lamb chops with olive oil and then sprinkle with salt and rosemary. Prepare the barbecue by heating to hot, about 450 degrees F. Turn the flame down. Cook the lamb chops 2 minutes on each side for rare—a minute longer if you like them medium. Allow to sit for at least 3 minutes before cutting. Serve with the salsa.

[SERVES 8]

Use either puff pastry or filo dough that is brushed with melted butter. This recipe may look intimidating, but it can be done in steps. It is really easy and the presentation is impressive.

Individual Beef en Croûte

MARINADE
1   cup dry white wine
¼   cup brandy
2   tablespoons olive oil
1   clove garlic, crushed
1   bay leaf
2   tablespoons finely chopped
    shallots

¼   teaspoon dried thyme
¼   teaspoon freshly ground pepper

6   (6-ounce) filet mignon steaks
Olive oil

MUSHROOM DUXELLES
2   tablespoons butter

2   tablespoons finely chopped
    shallots
2   cups finely chopped button
    mushrooms (about ½ pound)
½   teaspoon salt
Few grinds of fresh pepper
2   tablespoons Madeira wine
    (optional)

Menu suggestions

Artichokes Stuffed
with Seafood
(page 60)

Potato Nests and
Bean and Carrot Bundles
(page 117, 180)

Frozen Lemon Soufflé
Cake or Lemon Alaska
(pages 221, 205)

Wine suggestions

Syrah/Zinfandel

MARINADE
1. Place all the marinade ingredients in a plastic zip-lock bag. Add the steaks, refrigerate and marinate overnight or for at least 6 hours.
2. Remove from the marinade and pat dry on a paper towel. Brush with olive oil and quickly sear on a very hot grill or in a very hot frying pan just until each side is sealed. Place the filets on a cooling rack with a plate underneath them, cool and then refrigerate until chilled. Can be done up to 24 hours in advance.

MUSHROOM DEXELLES
3. Melt the butter in a medium frying pan and add the shallots. Put the mushrooms in a cotton towel and twist it to squeeze out as

much liquid as possible. Add to the pan to cook. Sprinkle in the salt and pepper and add the wine if using. Cook until all the juices have evaporated. Pour into a bowl and chill.

PASTRY
4. Defrost the pastry overnight in the refrigerator. Keep it cool to make it easy to work with.
5. Preheat the oven to 425 degrees F. Sprinkle a workspace with flour. Roll the pastry out until it is about 1/8 inch thick. Cut into 6 squarish pieces. In the center of each piece, spoon 1/6 of the mushroom mixture. Top with a chilled piece of filet. Mix the egg yolk with the water. Brush the edges of the pastry with the egg wash and seal them together around the beef. Cut off any extra pastry. Put the beef,

PASTRY

1 pound frozen puff pastry (2 sheets), thawed
¼ cup all-purpose flour
1 egg yolk
1 tablespoon water

MADEIRA SAUCE

8 tablespoons butter, divided
¾ cup frozen pearl onions
¾ cup button mushroom chunks (cut each mushroom into 6 pieces)
4 tablespoons flour
2 cups Beef Stock (page 73), heated in the microwave until hot
¼ cup Madeira (or 2 tablespoons red current jelly)
½ teaspoon salt
¼ teaspoon white pepper

seam side down, onto a parchment-lined baking sheet. Brush with the egg wash and decorate with any leftover pastry. Put into the freezer for 10 minutes.

6. Cook the beef in the oven for 15 to 20 minutes, or until the pastry is lightly browned and the internal temperature of the meat is 120 degrees F. Allow meat to sit for 5 minutes before serving. Serve with Madeira Sauce.

MADEIRA SAUCE

Melt 2 tablespoons butter in a small frying pan. Add the onions (no need to defrost them). Cook until they have browned and caramelized, about 5 minutes. Set aside. In the same pan, melt another 2 tablespoons butter and sauté the mushrooms until they have released their juices and the liquid has evaporated, about 7 minutes.

7. In a medium saucepan, melt the remaining butter. Add the flour and cook for 1 minute. Whisk in the hot stock and bring to a boil. Lower the heat and add the Madeira or jam, salt and pepper. If using canned beef stock, be careful about how much salt you use. Taste for seasonings. Add the mushroom and onions.

HINT: You can substitute unsweetened apple juice for the wine and brandy in the marinade.

[MAKES 6 SERVINGS]

Moussaka

3 eggplants
2 tablespoons salt, divided
½ cup olive oil, divided
2 cups finely chopped onion
2 pounds ground lamb
1 cup red wine
8 ripe plum tomatoes, skinned and seeded
1 teaspoon honey
1 cup Beef Stock (page 73)
1 cup chopped parsley, leaves only
2 tablespoons ground cinnamon
1 tablespoon dried oregano, crumbled
1 teaspoon ground allspice
1½ teaspoons salt
Freshly ground pepper

BECHAMEL SAUCE
4 tablespoons butter
¼ cup flour
2 cups milk, heated
¾ teaspoon grated nutmeg
1 bay leaf
1 cup grated Swiss cheese
1 cup small-curd cottage cheese
¼ cup crumbled feta cheese
4 eggs
Salt and white pepper to taste
Chopped parsley to garnish
½ cup grated Parmesan cheese

Menu suggestions

Baby Greens with Pomegranate Seeds and Spiced Pecans
(page 88)

Individual Frozen Lime Cheesecakes
(page 224)

Wine suggestions

Zinfandel / Syrah

1. Slice the unpeeled eggplant into 1/4-inch-thick slices. Lay out on paper towels and sprinkle with 1 tablespoon salt. Allow to sit for 15 minutes. Turn over and sprinkle with the remaining salt and allow to sit for another 15 minutes covered with another layer of paper towels to absorb the moisture.

2. In a large frying pan over medium-high heat, heat 3 tablespoons olive oil. Add the onions and sauté until translucent, about 5 minutes. Add the ground lamb and break up any large pieces with a wooden spoon. Continue cooking until the meat is nicely browned. Add the wine and cook until reduced by half. Add the tomatoes and honey, then lower the heat and simmer for 10 minutes. Stir in the stock, parsley and spices; simmer partially covered for about 30 minutes. Do not dry out all the liquid.

3. Preheat the broiler. Pat the eggplant dry and brush each side with olive oil. Place on a baking sheet and put under the broiler until lightly browned. Turn over, brush the other side with olive oil and brown; set aside.

BECHAMEL SAUCE

4. Melt the butter in a medium saucepan, add the flour and cook, whisking for 1 minute. Stir in the heated milk, nutmeg and bay leaf. Bring to a boil and then take off the heat.

5. Combine the Swiss, cottage and feta cheeses, and then add to the white sauce. Taste, for salt and white pepper. In an electric, mixer beat the eggs until frothy and pale. Carefully stir into the sauce.

6. Preheat the oven to 350 degrees F.

7. In an 9 x 13-inch baking dish, put down a layer of eggplant, cover with some meat sauce and a thin layer of the cheese sauce. Repeat the layers, ending with the last of the cheese sauce. Sprinkle the top with the Parmesan cheese and bake for 45 minutes. Allow to sit for 10 to 20 minutes before serving to firm up. Sprinkle with chopped parsley and more Parmesan cheese.

[SERVES 8 TO 10]

This dish is also very good without the pastry crust. Wrapping the lamb chops in filo pastry is another great way to prepare this recipe. If using filo, lower the oven temperature to 375 degrees F and cook them for 10 to 12 minutes.

Lamb Loin Chops in Puff Pastry with Red Currant Sauce

6   lamb loin chops, trimmed of fat
4   tablespoons finely chopped herbs (tarragon, rosemary, parsley, basil)
Salt and freshly ground pepper
3   tablespoons vegetable oil
1½ pounds frozen puff pastry, thawed

1   egg yolk, beaten
1   tablespoon water

RED CURRANT SAUCE
2   tablespoons butter
⅓   cup finely chopped onion
½   cup sliced mushrooms

4   teaspoons crushed pink peppercorns
¾   cup Cabernet Sauvignon
¾   cup Beef Stock (page 73)
⅓   cup red currant jelly
Salt and pepper

1.   Preheat oven to 450 degrees F.
2.   Coat the lamb with herbs and season with salt and pepper. In a medium frying pan, heat the vegetable oil until very hot. Sear the lamb for 30 seconds on each side. Remove from heat and cool on a wire rack.
3.   On a floured surface, roll out the puff pastry to a 1/4 inch thickness and cut into 1/2-x-8-inch strips. Arrange the strips over the chops in a crisscross pattern pressing the ends together under the chop. Place on a baking sheet lined with parchment paper. Brush the pastry with a mixture of the egg yolk and water and bake in the oven for 8 to 10 minutes (depending on the thickness of the lamb). For medium lamb, the internal temperature should register 135 degrees F on an instant thermometer. Set aside to rest in a warm place for 5 minutes before serving.

RED CURRANT SAUCE
4.   Melt the butter in a small skillet and sauté the onion until wilted; add mushrooms and peppercorns. Mix in the wine, bring to a boil and reduce by half. Add the stock and jelly and stir until the jelly had dissolved. Season with salt and pepper, strain and serve alongside the lamb.

[SERVES 6]

This is so delicious with the olives and sun-dried tomatoes in the sauce. The anchovies are simply flavor enhancers and you do not taste them.

Mediterranean Roast Lamb

6   cloves garlic, roasted
1   teaspoon olive oil
1   (4- to 5-pound) leg of lamb, boned
Salt and pepper
3   tablespoons olive oil

SAUCE

1½ cups Beef or Vegetable Stock (pages 73 and 74), divided
1   cup chopped kalamata olives
½   cup chopped oil-cured olives
4   canned anchovies, rinsed and finely minced
2   tablespoons chopped sun-dried tomatoes in oil

2   tablespoons finely chopped parsley
1   tablespoon lemon juice
Freshly ground pepper
Pinch of cayenne pepper
2   teaspoons flour
2   teaspoons butter, softened
Salt and pepper to taste

1. To roast the garlic, preheat the oven to 375 degrees F.

2. Cut a square of foil, place the garlic in the center and drizzle with 1 teaspoon of olive oil. Twist to seal and cook in the oven for about 20 minutes. You can also use a garlic baker.

3. Open the leg of lamb and with a sharp, thin knife. Trim out all the fat, tendons and gristle. This is time-consuming but worth the effort when it comes to eating. The roast naturally cuts into 3 pieces. Squeeze the garlic from the skins and spread 2 cloves on each piece of meat and sprinkle with a little salt and pepper. Roll the lamb pieces up and tie with kitchen string.

4. In a frying pan, on top of the stove, heat the olive oil until hot. Add the lamb and brown on all sides. Put the lamb into a roasting pan and roast for 15 to 20 minutes or until the internal temperature reaches 135 degrees F on an instant thermometer. Take out of the oven and allow to sit for 5 minutes before slicing thinly.

SAUCE

5. Add 1 cup stock to the frying pan. Place over medium heat and add the olives, anchovies, sun-dried tomatoes, parsley, lemon juice and both peppers; simmer for 5 minutes. Work the flour and butter into a paste and add to the sauce. Bring to a boil to thicken slightly. When the lamb is cooked, add 1/2 cup stock to the pan, place over medium heat and, with a wooden spoon, scrape all the brown bits off the bottom of the pan. Add to the sauce. Taste for salt and pepper. Serve the sauce with the lamb.

[SERVES 8]

Menu suggestions

Seafood Soup with Garlic Aioli
(page 68)

Parmesan-Crusted Potatoes
(page 116)

Petit Beans and Peas with Mint Pesto
(page 140)

Banana-White Chocolate Bread Pudding
(page 230)

Wine suggestions

Sangiovese

Cocoa or chocolate and chiles are traditional ingredients in mole sauces.
Here they are used as a rub for the lamb rack.

Mole-Rubbed Roast Rack of Lamb with Tropical Fruit Salsa

MOLE RUB

3 teaspoons chipotle chile powder

3 tablespoons ancho chile powder

¼ cup kosher salt

2 tablespoons dried Mexican
   oregano, toasted in a frying pan

1 tablespoon cocoa powder

RACK OF LAMB

12 cloves garlic

¼ cup olive oil

2 racks of lamb, trimmed off
   most of the fat

Tropical Fruit Salsa (page 160)

1. In a small bowl mix together all of the rub ingredients and set aside.

2. Crush the garlic through a garlic press into the olive oil. Using a pastry brush, brush the lamb with the garlic-olive oil mixture. Sprinkle the rub all over the lamb racks and refrigerate for at least 1 hour or overnight to marinate.

3. Preheat oven to 400 degrees F. Roast the lamb racks for about 20 minutes, or until the internal temperature of the lamb reaches 130 degrees F for medium-rare. Allow to sit for 5 to 10 minutes before serving. Serve with the Tropical Fruit Salsa.

[SERVES 6]

Menu suggestions

Gazpacho with Shellfish
(page 66)

Cinnamon Rice
with Pine Nuts
(page 134)

Green Beans with Cherry
Tomatoes
(page 141)

Chilled Mexican
Chocolate Soufflé
(page 228)

Wine suggestions

Syrah

This recipe can be put to marinate early in the day and be ready to cook just before eating. With meats, you really do have to use an instant thermometer to cook them correctly.

Pork Tenderloin with Apple-Chile Sauce

MARINADE:
½ cup apple juice
⅓ cup soy sauce
¼ cup honey
4 cloves garlic, minced
1 tablespoon minced fresh ginger

1½ teaspoons dried English
    mustard
¼ teaspoon Worcestershire sauce
¼ cup dark rum

PORK TENDERLOIN
1 pork tenderloin, about 2 pounds
½ cup apple jelly

2 Granny Smith apples, peeled
    and sliced
1½ teaspoons chipotle chile,
    chopped with some adobo sauce
½ teaspoon dried thyme, crushed
    with a mortar and pestle
Pinch of nutmeg
1½ tablespoons lime juice

1. Mix all the marinade ingredients together and marinate the pork in a plastic bag overnight or for at least 6 hours.
2. Take the tenderloin out of the marinade and dry. Strain the marinade and return to a pot. Add the remaining ingredients to the pot and bring to a boil to cook the apples. Barbecue or broil the tenderloin until the internal temperature reaches 145 degrees F, basting 2 or 3 times with the marinade mixture.
3. Allow the meat to sit for 10 minutes and then slice thinly and serve with the sauce.

HINT: Pork will still be very lightly pink in the center, tender and quite safe to eat at 145 degrees F.

[SERVES 4]

Menu suggestions
Spiced Butternut Squash
Soup with Stilton Biscuits
(pages 70, 197)

Sweet Potato Puree
in Zucchini Boats
(page 120)

Pumpkin–Ginger
Cheesecake
(page 215)

Wine suggestions
Merlot

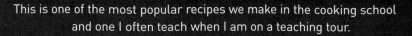
This is one of the most popular recipes we make in the cooking school and one I often teach when I am on a teaching tour.

Pork Loin with Dried Cranberry Sauce

2   whole pork tenderloins

MARINADE
2   onions, cut in half and thinly sliced
1   teaspoon minced fresh ginger
½   teaspoon ground cardamom
1   teaspoon ground cinnamon
½   teaspoon ground coriander
1½ teaspoons dried oregano

2   cloves garlic, minced
Juice of 2 oranges
Juice of 2 lemons
Salt and freshly ground pepper

DRIED CRANBERRY SAUCE
2   teaspoons butter
2   teaspoons flour
Strained reserved marinade
¼   cup firmly packed brown sugar

1   cup dry white wine
½   cup Chicken Stock (page 72)
1   teaspoon balsamic vinegar
½   cup dried cranberries
⅛   teaspoon dried tarragon, crumbled
Salt to taste
2   teaspoons minced fresh parsley
Parsley sprigs for garnish

Menu suggestions
Spiced Butternut Squash Soup with Stilton Biscuits
(pages 70, 197)

Potato and Leek Gratin
(page 130)

Green Beans with Cherry Tomatoes
(page 141)

Sweet Cheese Strudel
(page 218)

Wine suggestions
Pinot Noir
(Medium to Medium full)

1.   Remove the silver skin from the tenderloins and then place the tenderloins in a large plastic bag. Combine all of the marinade ingredients and pour over the pork. Cover and refrigerate for 6 hours, turning tenderloins 3 to 4 times. Remove from the refrigerator 30 minutes before roasting.

2.   Preheat oven to 375 degrees F. Remove the pork from the marinade, scrape off the onions and pat dry. Strain the marinade and reserve for the sauce. Roast the tenderloins for 20 minutes, or until the meat is pale pink when cut into the center or an instant thermometer reads 140 to 150 degrees F. Allow the meat to rest for 5 minutes. Cut the pork into 1/2-inch slices. Place the slices down the center of each dinner plate and spoon sauce around one side and garnish.

DRIED CRANBERRY SAUCE
3.   Melt the butter in a small saucepan and add the flour, whisking. Gradually add the marinade. Add brown sugar, wine and stock, whisking until the mixture is smooth. Add vinegar, cranberries, tarragon and salt. Bring to a boil, stirring occasionally and allowing the sauce to thicken, about 15 minutes. Stir in the parsley and simmer the sauce for 1 minute more. Serve the sauce hot and garnish with the sprigs of parsley.

[SERVES 6]

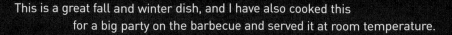

This is a great fall and winter dish, and I have also cooked this
for a big party on the barbecue and served it at room temperature.

Roast Pork Tenderloin Stuffed with Dried Fruit

FRUIT STUFFING
1½ cups Chicken Stock (page 72),
    divided
¼ cup dried tart cherries
¼ cup chopped dried apricots
¼ cup chopped dried apple
1 tablespoon dried currants

TENDERLOINS
1 tablespoon butter
1 medium shallot, chopped
¼ cup breadcrumbs
⅓ teaspoon dried thyme
⅓ teaspoon dried sage
½ teaspoon salt
Few grinds of fresh pepper
2 pork tenderloins
Salt and pepper

1 tablespoon butter
1 tablespoon vegetable oil

SAUCE
½ cup apple juice
2 teaspoons cornstarch
1 tablespoon water
¼ cup sweet dried cranberries
Salt and pepper to taste

Menu suggestions

Summer Vegetable Ravioli
(page 125)

Vegetable Couscous
(page 132)

Brandied Apple Mousse
(page 219)

Wine suggestions

Merlot

1. In a small saucepan over medium heat,
bring 1/2 cup of stock to a boil. Remove from
heat and add the cherries, apricots, apple and
currants. Allow to steep for 30 minutes. Strain
fruit, reserving the liquid, and press on the fruit
to extract as much liquid as possible.

2. In a small skillet over medium heat, melt 1
tablespoon butter and sauté the shallot until tender, about 3 minutes. Pour into a bowl with the
breadcrumbs, thyme, sage, salt and pepper. Mix
in the fruit.

3. Preheat the oven to 350 degrees F or heat up
the grill. On a cutting board with a sharp knife,
remove the silver skin and fat from the tenderloins. Make a cut along the length of each
tenderloin about two-thirds of the way through to
open them up. Cover with a sheet of parchment
or plastic wrap and pound with a meat pounder
until they are about 1/2 inch thick. Spread half
the stuffing over each tenderloin, roll up lengthwise and tie with kitchen string. Salt and pepper
the outside of the meat.

4. To roast, melt the 1 tablespoon butter in an
ovenproof pan and add oil over high heat. When
hot, add the tenderloins and turn every few minutes to brown all over. Add the reserved soaking
liquid from the fruit and 1 cup of stock to the
pan. Place in the oven uncovered and roast for
15 to 20 minutes, or until the internal temperature reaches 140 degrees F. Take the pork
tenderloin out of the pan and allow the meat to
rest for 5 minutes before cutting into it.

HEAD SAUCE

5. Pour the roasting liquids (stock and fruit
soaking liquid) into a saucepan. Add the apple
juice and bring to a boil. Soften the cornstarch in
the water and stir in along with the cranberries.
Boil to thicken and then taste for salt and
pepper.

6. Cut the strings from the roast, slice thinly,
spoon some of the sauce over the tenderloin and
serve the rest of the sauce in a bowl on the side.

[SERVES 6]

This recipe can also be made with thin turkey scaloppine or flattened chicken breasts.

Veal Rolls

8   thin slices veal scaloppine
    (1½ pounds)
2   tablespoons butter
4   shallots, finely chopped
1   clove garlic, minced
1   (6-ounce) package baby spinach
½   cup ricotta cheese
¼   teaspoon freshly grated nutmeg

½   cup freshly grated Parmesan
    cheese
½   teaspoon salt
⅛   teaspoon pepper
1   egg white, beaten until stiff
2   tablespoons butter
2   tablespoons vegetable oil

SAUCE
2   tablespoons butter

1   shallot, finely chopped
1   small clove garlic, minced
2   cups sliced mushrooms (oyster
    if available)
¼   cup dry white wine
¾   cup Chicken Stock (page 72)
¼   cup whipping cream
Salt and pepper to taste
½   cup chopped Italian parsley

1.   Between two sheets of parchment paper, pound the veal thin and even, being careful not to tear the meat.

2.   In a large frying pan over medium heat, melt the butter and add the shallots. Cook for about 3 minutes, add the garlic and cook for 1 minute. Add the baby spinach, cover and cook until the spinach has wilted. Transfer the spinach mixture to a strainer over a bowl to drain and cool.

3.   In a large bowl, mix together the ricotta, nutmeg, Parmesan cheese, salt and pepper. Roughly chop the drained spinach mixture and add to the cheese mixture.

4.   With an electric mixer, beat the egg white until stiff and add to the filling mixture.

5.   Lay out the veal and top the 8 pieces with the filling. Roll the meat around the filling, tucking in the ends. Secure with a toothpick or tie loosely with kitchen string.

6.   Preheat the oven to 350 degrees F.

7.   In a large frying pan over medium-high heat, melt the butter and the oil. When hot, add half the veal rolls and brown quickly on each side. Put into a greased ovenproof pan. Brown the remaining rolls. Place veal rolls into the oven and cook for 10 minutes.

SAUCE
8.   Using the same unwashed frying pan, melt the butter and sauté the shallot for 2 minutes. Add the garlic and cook for 1 minute. Add the mushrooms and sauté until wilted and their juices have almost evaporated. Pour in the wine and boil until almost evaporated, about 1 minute. Add the stock and cook for 3 minutes. Stir in the cream, taste for salt and pepper. Finally, stir in the parsley and any juices from the cooked veal.

9.   Slice the veal into 3 pieces and serve with some of the sauce.

[SERVES 8]

Menu suggestions

Spinach Ravioli with
Chile-Tomato
Cream Sauce
(page 50)

Creamy Polenta
(page 134)

Sautéed Mushrooms
with Spinach
(page 144)

Buttermilk Panna Cotta
(page 209)

Wine suggestions

Sangiovese or Zinfandel

Baking

Unlike cooking, which is an art and allows a lot of variation, baking is a science in which the measurements need to be exact. When measuring flour, spoon the flour into the dry-ingredient measuring cup and level off with a knife. Scooping up the flour with the measuring cup compacts the flour and gives you more flour than the recipe needs. Make sure you use a dry-ingredient measuring cup you can level off, not a wet-ingredient measuring cup that has a lip for pouring. Yes, you do need two kinds of measuring cups! Spoon measurements should be leveled-off spoonfuls. When using baking recipes from other books where the dry measurements are in pounds or ounces, you must weigh your dry ingredients on a scale. I have converted all the dry ingredients in this book into cups and spoonfuls. This is why some recipes have, for example, 1 cup plus two tablespoons of an ingredient. If you bake in glass pans or use the convection bake setting on your oven, lower the oven temperature by 25 degrees F.

We make these in many of our Southwestern classes. If you do not have a cast-iron corn stick pan you can make these in a mini cupcake pan or a cast-iron skillet. The sticks in the skillet will need to cook for 20 minutes.

Chile-Corn Sticks

¼ cup vegetable oil, plus more to grease the pan

2 eggs

1 cup buttermilk

1½ cups grated sharp cheddar cheese

1 (8-ounce) can cream-style corn

1¼ cups chopped red onion

3 fresh jalapenos, seeded and finely chopped

1 cup white cornmeal

½ cup unbleached flour

2 teaspoons baking powder

½ teaspoon baking soda

½ teaspoon salt

1. Preheat the oven to 400 degrees F. Oil the corn stick pan (or cast-iron skillet) and heat in the oven until the oil is sizzling hot.

2. In a medium bowl, whisk the eggs. Add the oil and buttermilk. Stir in the cheese, corn, onion and jalapenos.

3. In a large bowl, mix together the cornmeal, flour, baking powder, baking soda and salt. Stir the egg mixture into the dry ingredients. Blend well but do not over-stir the batter.

4. Remove the cornbread pan from the oven and fill each one halfway with batter. Cook for 10 to 12 minutes or until the top of the sticks are browned and they have slightly shrunk away from the sides of the pan. Allow to cool for 5 minutes before removing from the pan.

HINT: They freeze well in a container that protects them from breaking. Refresh them for a few minutes in the oven if they have been frozen.

[MAKES 16 BREADSTICKS]

Grandmother's Bran Cookies

1 cup butter, softened

¾ cup sugar

1 egg

1 cup flour

1 cup whole wheat flour

1 cup bran

2 teaspoons baking powder

¼ teaspoon salt

1. Preheat the oven to 350 degrees F.

2. In an electric mixer, cream together the butter and sugar; add the egg. In a bowl, mix together the dry ingredients, and then slowly add the dry ingredients to the butter mixture.

On a floured board, roll mixture out thinly and cut into 2-inch rounds with a cookie cutter. Put rounds onto a baking sheet lined with parchment paper or a silicone baking sheet and cook for 10 to 12 minutes, or until medium brown.

[MAKES 2 1/2 DOZEN COOKIES]

These are plain cookies that are good with a cup of tea. I also like to serve them as an appetizer topped with whipped cream cheese, a slice of peeled fresh peach and a mint leaf. They are also good with whipped cream cheese and fig jam or chutney.

Nothing is better than fresh bread. Use this as part of your meal or split it in half to make great sandwiches and panini. You can also use rosemary, olives, cheese, sun-dried tomatoes or sesame seeds as a topping.

Basic Focaccia

DOUGH

2 packages yeast

1 teaspoon sugar

2 cups warm water (at no more than 110 degrees F)

5½ cups bread flour

3 tablespoons olive oil

1 teaspoon salt

TOPPING

1 red onion, sliced

2 cloves garlic, crushed

1 tablespoon fresh rosemary leaves, left whole

2 tablespoons olive oil

3 tablespoons grated Parmesan cheese

1 tablespoon coarse salt

1. In the bowl of an electric mixer with a dough hook, mix the yeast, sugar and water together for 30 seconds. Allow to sit undisturbed for about 5 minutes to ensure the yeast is active. You will see the mixture begin to bubble; this is called "proofing" the yeast.
2. Mix in half the flour. Add the olive oil and mix for another 30 seconds. Add salt and enough of the remaining flour to make a medium-soft dough that is slightly sticky. Mix well for about 5 minutes. Turn dough onto a lightly floured board and knead until the dough is smooth and no longer sticky. Place in a large oiled bowl, turning the dough to oil all sides, cover with plastic wrap and let rise in a warm place for about 1 hour, or until it doubles in bulk. (Note: To make dough by hand, follow the above but mix in bowl with a wooden spoon. When more than three-fourths of flour has been added, incorporate the rest by kneading it in.)
3. Preheat oven to 400 degrees F.
4. Press risen dough evenly into an oiled 15 1/2 x 10 1/2 x 1-inch baking sheet. Let rise for 30 minutes. With your fingers, dimple dough, making 1/4-inch-deep indentations. Spread on the topping.

TOPPING
5. Mix together the onion, garlic, rosemary and olive oil. Spread over the bread and then sprinkle Parmesan cheese and salt over top. Bake for 30 minutes; allow to sit for 10 minutes before cutting.

HINT: If you use rapid-rise yeast this bread can be done in half the time.

[MAKES 18]
2 1/2-inch-square pieces

These biscuits (also called scones) can also be made appetizer-size, split in half and topped with smoked turkey or ham and a little chutney. They are best used the day they are made.

Stilton Biscuits

2½ cups all-purpose flour
2 tablespoons sugar
1 tablespoon baking powder
¾ teaspoon cream of tartar

½ teaspoon salt
½ cup unsalted butter, well chilled
1 cup grated extra-sharp cheese, well chilled

½ cup Stilton cheese, crumbled (can also use other blue cheeses)
1¼ cups buttermilk, well chilled
1 egg

1. Preheat the oven to 400 degrees F. Line a baking sheet with parchment paper or a silicone sheet liner.
2. In a large bowl, mix together the flour, sugar, baking powder, cream of tartar and salt. Cut the butter into very small cubes and with your fingertips rub the butter into the flour mixture until it resembles coarse meal.

Mix in the cheeses. Whisk the buttermilk and the egg in a small bowl. Pour into the flour mixture, and then gently and quickly mix together. Using a 2-inch ice cream scoop, scoop the dough into the baking sheet about 2 inches apart. Bake for 12 to 15 minutes, or until golden brown.

[MAKES 12 BISCUITS]

Orange Shortbread Cookies

1 cup salted butter at room temperature

Zest of 1 medium orange
1 cup powdered sugar

2 cups flour
Pinch of salt

1. Preheat the oven to 350 degrees F.
2. Chop the butter into pieces and put into a medium bowl. With a wooden spoon, mix in the orange zest and then the powdered sugar. Rub in the flour and salt until it resembles coarse sand. Knead the dough gently into a soft ball.

3. On a floured surface, roll a small spoonful into a ball. Put onto a baking sheet lined with parchment paper or a silicone baking mat. Flatten with a fork dipped in cold water. Bake for 10 to 12 minutes, or until very lightly browned.

[MAKES ABOUT 40 COOKIES]

These are traditional shortbread with the flavor of citrus. You can use lemon or tangerine zest to change the flavor. They go great with a cup of coffee.

The Best Chocolate Chip Oatmeal Cookies

1 cup brown sugar, firmly packed
1 cup white sugar
1 cup unsalted butter
2 large eggs

2 teaspoons vanilla
½ teaspoon salt
1 teaspoon baking soda
2 cups all-purpose flour

2½ cups quick-cook oatmeal
1¼ cups chocolate chips
1½ cups chopped walnuts

1. Preheat the oven to 400 degrees F.
2. Using an electric mixer, cream together the sugars and butter until smooth and creamy. Beat in the eggs, one at a time, and scrape down the sides of the bowl. Add the vanilla.
3. In a medium bowl, mix together the salt, baking soda, flour and oatmeal. Carefully mix the dry ingredients into the butter mixture. Add the chocolate chips and nuts. Place small spoonfuls 2 inches apart on a parchment-lined baking sheet and bake for 15 minutes. Allow the cookies to cool on the pan before removing.

[MAKES 48 COOKIES]

Queen Elizabeth Cake

1 cup boiling water
1 cup chopped dates
½ cup butter
1 cup sugar

1 egg
1 teaspoon vanilla
1 cup all-purpose flour
½ cup cake flour
1 teaspoon baking powder
Pinch of salt
1 teaspoon baking soda

TOPPING
¾ cup brown sugar
¾ cup shredded, sweetened coconut
4 tablespoons butter
5 tablespoons cream
¾ cup walnuts, chopped

1. Preheat the oven to 350 degrees F. Butter and flour an 9 x 13-inch baking pan.
2. Pour the boiling water over the dates.
3. Using an electric mixer, beat the butter and sugar until well blended. Beat in the egg and vanilla. Sift the flours, baking powder and salt. Slowly blend into the butter and egg mixture. Add the baking soda to the date mixture and mix into the cake batter. Pour into the prepared pan and bake for 35 to 40 minutes.

TOPPING
4. For the topping, mix the brown sugar, coconut, butter and cream in a saucepan. Boil for 5 minutes and then stir in the walnuts. Spread over the warm cake.

[MAKES 24 (2-INCH-SQUARE) PIECES]

This cake is usually made in a rectangular baking pan and cut into squares. It could also be made into a layer cake using two 7-inch-round pans and using the topping to fill and top the cake.

Desserts

What is a meal without a sweet ending? Dessert can simply be fruit with ice cream or yogurt, or a fabulous chilled soufflé. It can be something decadently chocolate or a sweet sauce that goes over whatever is available. I suggest you balance your meal with dessert. If it is a heavy meal, you probably want a light dessert. The season of year can also influence the sort of dessert you serve. When the weather is cold, you may feel more like a heavier dessert. Summer produces a variety of fresh fruit and berries to be enjoyed in numerous ways. The Chocolate Pecan Tart with Carmel Sauce on page 212 is one of my favorites to make ahead of time and freeze (in the tart pan because the crust is fragile). Dessert sauces can also be frozen so they're ready to use. It is a good feeling to know that an impressive dessert is already in the freezer when you have unexpected guests.

This dessert will freeze after cooking. Be careful to protect it because the crust is fragile and will break up. This recipe is for use with a full 9 x 14-inch sheet of filo. If you have the smaller-sized sheets, the recipe will make two strudels.

Apple Strudel

4 cups sliced Granny Smith apples, about 4 apples
½ cup butter, melted
½ cup dried breadcrumbs, toasted
1 cup raisins

Zest of 1 lemon
½ cup walnuts (or pecans)
1 cup sugar
2 teaspoons cinnamon

6 large sheets of filo (or 12 small sheets) defrosted in the refrigerator overnight
¼ cup butter, melted
Powdered sugar to garnish

1. Peel, core and slice the apples. Put into a large bowl and pour the 1/2 cup melted butter over top. Stir in the breadcrumbs, raisins, lemon zest and walnuts. Mix the sugar with the cinnamon and add to the apples.

2. On a clean, dry work surface, open the filo and cover with a sheet of parchment paper and a lightly dampened towel. Working with 1 filo sheet at a time on a silicone baking sheet or parchment paper, brush the melted butter over the sheets of filo and lay one on top of another. After you have layered 6 buttered sheets, spoon the apple filling along the cen-

ter. With the help of the silicone mat, roll the filo over the filling to form a long log. Slide onto a rimmed baking sheet. Refrigerate to set the butter.

3. Preheat the oven to 400 degrees F.

4. With a sharp knife, score the top of the filo into serving slices. Bake in the center of the oven for 35 to 40 minutes, lowering the temperature if the filo begins to brown too much. Cool and sprinkle with powdered sugar before serving. Serve with sweetened whipped cream or vanilla ice cream.

[SERVES 12]

This dessert resembles strawberry shortcake, a good family dessert that does not have the usual liquor in it. If you cannot find ladyfingers, use a frozen angel food cake cut into fingers. Freezing the cake makes it easier to handle.

Strawberry Tiramisu

1 cup boiling water
⅓ cup sugar
1 (10-ounce) package frozen strawberries, thawed

1½ packages (7 ounces) ladyfingers
1 (8-ounce) container mascarpone cheese
2 tablespoons sugar

1½ cups heavy cream, whipped
1 teaspoon vanilla extract
3 cups fresh strawberries, hulled and thinly sliced
Chocolate shavings to decorate

1. Pour the boiling water over the sugar and stir to dissolve.

2. Put the thawed strawberries into a food processor or blender, along with the sugar syrup, and blend well. Strain the strawberries through a sieve set over a bowl and gently press on the solids; discard the solids.

3. Quickly dip a third of the ladyfingers into the strawberry syrup, turning to coat lightly. Lay ladyfingers on the bottom of an 8 x 10-inch serving dish.

4. With an electric mixer, whisk the mascarpone and 2 tablespoons sugar to blend. In another bowl, whip the cream and vanilla until stiff, and then fold into the mascarpone mixture.

5. Spoon one-third of the mascarpone cream mixture over the ladyfingers and smooth. Sprinkle with half the sliced strawberries. Dip more ladyfingers into the syrup to form another layer.

6. Spoon one-third of the cream on top and sprinkle with the remaining strawberries. Dip a final layer of ladyfingers and spread the remaining cream on top. Cover and chill at least 4 hours or overnight. Decorate with chocolate shavings.

[SERVES 8]-

Make and freeze the mousse at least a day ahead so that it is firm enough to work with. Once the meringue is covering the mousse it can stay in the freezer for up to 3 days, well covered, before being browned in the oven.

Lemon Alaska

FROZEN LEMON CURD MOUSSE
⅔ cup lemon juice
Zest of 2 lemons
6 tablespoons butter
½ cup sugar

3 yolks
1 egg
1¼ cups cream

LEMON ALASKA
1 frozen pound cake or angel food cake
¼ cup orange marmalade
3 egg whites, at room temperature
½ cup sugar

1. Using a double boiler, or a metal bowl over a pot of simmering water, mix together the lemon juice, lemon zest, butter, sugar, egg yolks and egg. Stir over medium-low heat until the curd thickens and a small amount of steam rises off the curd; strain and chill until cold by placing it in a bowl set over another bowl filled with ice and a small amount of water.

2. Whip the cream to moderately firm peaks. Fold a third of the cream at a time into the curd. Line 10 muffin tins with plastic wrap, fill each muffin with the mousse. Cover and freeze for at least 4 hours.

3. For the Alaska, slice the pound cake into ten 1/2-inch slices. With a 2-inch-round cookie cutter, cut the sliced pound cake into 10 circles. Melt the marmalade and brush it gen-

erously over the top side of the cake circles. Place 1 piece of cake, marmalade side down, on each lemon mousse. Return to the freezer.

4. With an electric mixer, beat the egg whites to stiff peaks. Gradually beat in the sugar, 1 tablespoon at a time, to make a glossy meringue. Turn the mousses out of the pans and remove the plastic wrap. Cover each dessert completely with some of the meringue. Refreeze for up to 3 days.

5. Preheat oven to 450 degrees F. (Bake at 425 degrees F if you have convection setting.) Place desserts on a baking sheet and bake for 4 minutes, or until the meringue just starts to brown. Serve immediately, either alone or with Raspberry Sauce (see page 226) and fresh berries to decorate the plate.

HINT: You can freeze the mousse in an ice cream freezer and make delicious gelato.

[SERVES 10]

This is quite a spectacular dessert and not at all difficult to make.
Serve the frosted shells with the orange top alongside as a decoration.
You can also sugarcoat the tops.

Chocolate Mousse in Orange Shells

8   medium oranges
2   egg whites
1   cup sugar

CHOCOLATE MOUSSE
4   ounces good-quality semi-

sweet chocolate, chopped
1   tablespoon gelatin
1   cup milk
4   eggs, separated
¼   cup sugar
½   cup whipping cream, whipped

1   tablespoon orange liqueur

CHOCOLATE LEAVES
1   ounce dark chocolate
8   small citrus leaves

1. Find out how the oranges sit in their most stable position. Cut the top quarter off the orange and set aside. With a grapefruit spoon, carefully scoop out the insides. Lightly beat the 2 egg whites to soft peaks and paint the outside of the orange shells with the egg whites. Sprinkle thickly with the sugar so the outside of the orange is covered. Set the oranges aside to set. This can be done a day in advance so long as there is no humidity.

2. For the mousse, cut the chocolate into small pieces about the size of chocolate chips with a large knife.

3. Dissolve the gelatin in the milk. In the microwave, bring the milk mixture to a simmer, about 1 minute. Whisk the egg yolks with the sugar. Slowly pour the hot milk mixture into the egg mixture. Pour into a medium saucepan and over medium heat cook until almost boiling (it coats the back of the spoon and you will see a small vapor of steam begin

to rise). Do not boil. Take off the heat and add the chocolate; stir until melted.

4. Pour into a clean medium bowl sitting in another bowl full of ice and a little water. Chill filling until it is almost set.

5. Using an electric mixer, beat the egg whites until stiff. In another bowl, beat the cream with the orange liqueur. Fold the cream into the almost-set, chilled chocolate mixture, and then gently fold the egg whites into the chocolate mixture. Fill the orange shells with the mixture and allow to set for at least 2 hours. Decorate with Chocolate Leaves.

CHOCOLATE LEAVES

6. Melt dark chocolate carefully in the microwave. Spread the top of citrus leaves with the melted chocolate and chill to set. Peel the citrus leaf off the chocolate and place the chocolate leaf in the top of the orange.

[SERVES 8]

By poaching the fruit and adding a sweet syrupy sauce, you have a
cross between a sauce and a salsa. This salsa can be used with many desserts.

Poached Fruit Salsa

1 mango, peeled	1 cup seeded watermelon	½ cup apple juice
1 kiwifruit, peeled	3 tablespoons unsalted butter	½ cup honey
1 cup fresh pineapple	1 tablespoon dark rum, prefer-	3 tablespoons lemon juice
	ably spiced	½ cup sweetened coconut

1. Cut all the fruit into 1/2-inch dice. In a medium frying pan, melt the butter until it sizzles. Add the fruit and cook until it has slightly softened, about 2 minutes. Use a slotted spoon to transfer the fruit to a glass bowl and chill.

2. Add the rum, apple juice, honey and lemon juice to the frying pan. Simmer about 10 minutes until the sauce is thick, syrupy and reduced to about 1/2 cup. Pour over the fruit and chill.

3. In a small, dry frying pan over medium heat, toast the coconut, shaking the pan often until it is gently browned. Sprinkle over the plated dessert to garnish.

[MAKES 4 CUPS]

Panna cotta should have just enough gelatin to make it gently set. I prefer to serve it in martini glasses rather than to put it into a small ramekin and unmold it onto a plate, with fruit spooned around it.

Buttermilk Panna Cotta

2 tablespoons water	1½ cups whipping cream	2 cups buttermilk
1 tablespoon gelatin	½ cup sugar	1 teaspoon vanilla

1. Put the water into a small measuring cup, sprinkle over the gelatin and allow to soften for 5 minutes.

2. In a small saucepan, mix together the cream and sugar. Heat over medium heat until the sugar has dissolved—do not boil. Remove from the heat and stir in the gelatin mixture.

3. Fill a large bowl with about 6 cups of ice and 1 cup of water. Place the mixture in a smaller bowl that is placed in the larger bowl filled with ice. Stir until the mixture has cooled to warm. Stir in the buttermilk and the vanilla. Pour into 8 martini glasses or dessert bowls. Refrigerate for 6 hours or overnight to set. Serve topped with Poached Fruit Salsa (opposite), or a mixture of fresh berries.

[SERVES 8]

A good cool-weather dessert that is a different presentation to apple pie.
If you prefer, you can use store-bought caramel topping in this recipe.

Individual Caramel Apple Puddings

1½ pounds Granny Smith apples, peeled, cored and thinly sliced
⅓ cup water
2 tablespoons sugar
2 whole cloves

CARAMEL
3 tablespoons water
½ teaspoon lemon juice
¾ cup sugar

SPONGE TOPPING
6 tablespoons butter, at room temperature

½ cup sugar
1 teaspoon vanilla
2 eggs
1 cup flour
1 teaspoon baking powder
¼ cup milk

1. Put the apple slices, water, sugar and cloves in a saucepan and simmer until the apples are tender, about 10 minutes. Remove the cloves. Divide apples between 8 (6-ounce) ramekins.

2. Preheat oven to 350 degrees F.

CARMEL
3. For the caramel, add the water, lemon juice and then the sugar to a small frying pan. Over medium-high heat cook the mixture, without stirring, until the sugar turns to a light caramel color. Quickly pour over the apple mixture in the ramekins. Put into the oven to heat up while you prepare the topping.

SPONGE TOPPING
4. Cream the butter, sugar and vanilla with an electric mixer until fluffy. Add the eggs one at a time, beating between each addition. Sift the flour and baking powder and gently fold into the egg mixture along with the milk. Spoon onto the top of the hot apple mixture and return to the oven for 25 to 30 minutes, or until a toothpick comes out clean. Serve with scoops of vanilla ice cream.

[SERVES 8]

Chocolate and caramel sound so decadent. Because they are both so sweet, they complement each other well. Use good-quality chocolate in all your desserts or they will have a grainy quality to them. Both the tart and the sauce can be made ahead and frozen.

Chocolate Pecan Tart with Caramel Sauce

TART
2   cups pecans
¼   cup golden brown sugar, firmly packed
¼   teaspoon cinnamon
2   tablespoons unsalted butter, at room temperature

9- inch-round tart pan with a removable bottom
Powdered sugar for garnish

FILLING
¾   cup whipping cream
16   ounces (1 pound) bittersweet or semisweet chocolate

CARAMEL SAUCE
½   cup unsalted butter
1   cup plus 3 tablespoons sugar
2   cups whipping cream

1. Preheat the oven to 325 degrees F.
2. Using a food processor, grind the pecans with the brown sugar and cinnamon until they resemble coarse meal. Add the butter and mix just to blend. Press the nut mixture into the bottom and up the sides of the tart pan. Bake in the oven until golden brown, about 20 minutes. Transfer to a cooling rack and pour in the filling; smooth out the top. Refrigerate for 2 hours, or until the filling has set.

FILLING
3. Bring the cream to a simmer in a small saucepan. Add the chocolate and stir until melted. Pour into the pecan crust.
4. To serve, sprinkle the top of the tart with powdered sugar and cut into wedges. Serve with some sauce drizzled over the top.

CARAMEL SAUCE
5. Use an 11-inch frying pan to melt the butter. Add the sugar and cook over medium-high heat, stirring occasionally with a wooden spoon until it turns a medium golden brown (about the color of dark brown sugar). Heat the cream in the microwave until hot while the sugar is cooking. As soon as the sugar has turned golden, turn off the heat and slowly add the heated cream. The mixture will bubble up and the sugar will set around the spoon in a lump of soft toffee. Put back over medium heat, bring to a boil and cook until the toffee/sugar has dissolved into the sauce. Sauce keeps for 2 weeks in the refrigerator or can be frozen. Microwave it until slightly warm before using.

[SERVES 8]

The sensation of the cold, smooth chocolate ice cream in your mouth, followed by a slow building of the chile heat when you swallow, is quite delicious. If you are not used to eating chiles, start with one chile.

Chocolate-Chile Ice Cream

1 or 2 habanero chiles, seeded and finely chopped
2 cups milk

12 ounces semisweet or bitter-sweet chocolate, chopped
9 large egg yolks

1 cup sugar
2 cups whipping cream, well chilled
2 tablespoons vanilla

1. In a medium saucepan, mix together the chiles and the milk. Over medium heat, bring to a simmer. Take off the heat and stir in the chopped chocolate. Stir until the chocolate has melted. Allow it to sit for 10 minutes to infuse the chile flavor.

2. Make an ice bath by pouring about 6 cups of ice cubes and 1 cup of water into a large bowl. Set a slightly smaller bowl on top of the ice to chill. Pour 2 cups of cream into the bowl to chill.

3. In another bowl, whisk the egg yolks and the sugar together. Whisking well, add to the chocolate mixture. Over medium-low heat, whisk the mixture until it thickens slightly. It should coat the back of the spoon and you

should see just a wisp of steam rising. Be careful not to get the mixture too hot and scramble the eggs. Strain through a fine strainer into the chilled bowl of cream that is over ice so it cools down. Add the vanilla.

4. If you are using an ice cream machine, stir well and as soon as the mixture is cold, freeze it in the machine following the manufacturer's instructions.

HINT:If you do not have a machine, whip the chilled 2 cups cream and vanilla to soft peaks before adding the chocolate mixture. When the chocolate mixture has chilled, fold together with the whipped cream and freeze.

HINT: My students and staff are divided about the number of chiles to use in this recipe. I prefer to use two chiles.

[SERVES 10]

This is a perfect fall cheesecake and a delicious alternative to pumpkin pie for the holidays.

Pumpkin-Ginger Cheesecake

CRUST
1 cup ginger cookie crumbs
⅓ cup sugar
½ cup butter, melted

FILLING
4 (8-ounce) packages cream cheese at room temperature
2 cups sugar
2 cups canned pumpkin
¼ cup flour
6 large eggs, whisked together
Zest of 1 lemon
¼ cup sour cream

TOPPING
1 cup whipping cream
2 tablespoons powdered sugar
½ teaspoon vanilla
3 ounces candied ginger, chopped

CRUST

1. In a food processor, mix the cookie crumbs with the sugar and the butter. Press into the bottom and a half inch up the sides of a 9-inch springform pan to form the crust.

2. Preheat the oven to 400 degrees F.

FILLING

3. Blend together the cream cheese, sugar, pumpkin, flour, eggs, lemon zest and sour cream in an electric mixer bowl. Pour into the pan with the crust and set on a baking sheet.

Bake for 15 minutes at 400 degrees F and then reduce the heat to 225 degrees F. Bake for 1 1/2 hours, or until set. Allow to cool completely and then refrigerate overnight.

TOPPING

4. Unmold from the pan. Using an electric mixer, whip the cream with the powdered sugar and vanilla. Spoon the cream into a piping bag and decorate the top of the cheesecake. Sprinkle with the candied ginger.

[SERVES 12]

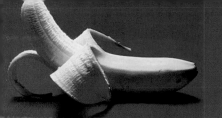

Crêpes with Caramelized Bananas and Mexican Chocolate Ice Cream

CREPE BATTER

2   cups whole milk
3   large eggs
½   teaspoon ground cinnamon
⅛   teaspoon ground cloves
1½ tablespoons sugar
2   teaspoons vanilla

¼   teaspoon salt
1   cup all-purpose flour
3   tablespoons butter, melted

FILLING

1   cup slivered almonds
4   tablespoons unsalted butter

4   ripe bananas, skinned and sliced
⅓   cup sugar
½   cup whipping cream, heated in the microwave
1   tablespoon dark rum

CREPE BATTER

1. In a blender or food processor, blend the milk, eggs, cinnamon, cloves, sugar, vanilla and salt until smooth. With machine running, add the flour 1 heaping tablespoon at a time, blending well after each addition. Blend in the melted butter and then strain batter into a bowl. Allow to stand 2 hours at room temperature.

2. Heat an 8-inch nonstick skillet or crêpe pan over medium-high heat and brush with a thin coating of melted butter. Pour 2 generous tablespoons of batter into skillet and swirl to coat bottom. Cook until bottom of crêpe is light brown, about 30 seconds. Loosen edges gently with spatula. Carefully turn crêpe over and cook the other side for about another minute; transfer to a plate. Repeat with remaining batter, brushing skillet with melted butter as needed and stacking crêpes. Can be made 1 day ahead. Cover and chill, but bring to room temperature before filling.

FILLING

3. Put the almonds in a small, dry frying pan and lightly brown over medium heat, shaking the pan at regular intervals. Take off the heat and cool in a bowl.

4. Melt the butter in a large pan. Fry the bananas until golden brown on each side. Take out of the pan and keep warm. Add the sugar to the pan and stir very gently until it turns a light caramel color. Add the cream and stir until blended. Stir in the bananas and the rum.

5. Fill each crêpe with some of the banana mixture and roll up or fold. Place 2 on a plate, top with a scoop of Mexican Chocolate Ice Cream (see page 220) and sprinkle with the toasted almonds.

[SERVES 8]

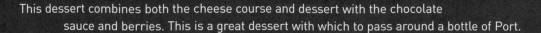

This dessert combines both the cheese course and dessert with the chocolate sauce and berries. This is a great dessert with which to pass around a bottle of Port.

Sweet Cheese Strudel

1 (8-ounce) package cream cheese, at room temperature
1 cup ricotta cheese
1 tablespoon lemon zest
1 tablespoon lemon juice
¼ cup sugar
1 egg, separated

¼ cup golden raisins (or mini chocolate chips)
¼ cup blanched almonds, ground
½ package filo (about 10 sheets)
1 stick butter, melted
Powdered sugar to garnish
Fresh berries to garnish

CHOCOLATE SAUCE
6 ounces good-quality semisweet chocolate, chopped
1 cup heavy cream
⅛ teaspoon salt
½ cup sugar
4 tablespoons butter

1. In an electric mixer bowl, beat the cheeses together. Add the lemon zest, juice and sugar. Beat until blended. Add the egg yolk, scraping down the sides of the bowl, mixing until just blended. Fold in the raisins and the almonds.

2. Preheat the oven to 350 degrees F.

3. Open the filo and cover with a sheet of parchment and a lightly dampened towel. Working 1 sheet at a time, separate the filo and place it on the parchment paper. Brush the filo sheet completely and quickly with the melted butter. Repeat with another sheet of filo, layering one sheet on top of another until you have at least 10 sheets on top of each other.

4. In a clean mixer bowl, beat the egg white until it is fluffy and forms soft peaks. Fold the egg white into the egg yolk mixture. Spoon the mixture along the long side of the filo. Using the parchment paper to help, roll the filo with the mixture inside, folding in each end, into a strudel. Brush well with butter.

5. Using the parchment paper, carefully lift onto a baking sheet. With a sharp knife score the top

layers of the filo into serving-size slices. (Do not cut all the way through the top of the filo.) Bake for about 35 minutes, or until the filo is lightly browned. Cool to room temperature (the filo will soften if it is refrigerated) and sprinkle with powdered sugar before serving. Serve with fresh berries and chocolate sauce.

6. For the sauce, combine all the ingredients in a saucepan and warm over low heat until the chocolate has melted. Remove from heat and serve.

HINT: If you use smaller-sized sheets of filo, you will make 2 strudels. (See Apple Strudel, page 202).

VARIATIONS: Add once the sauce has been taken off the heat:

FOR CHOCOLATE ORANGE SAUCE add 1 tablespoon orange zest and 2 tablespoons orange liqueur or orange juice.

FOR CHOCOLATE MINT SAUCE add 1 teaspoon mint extract or 2 tablespoons minted liqueur.

[SERVES 10 TO 12]

A light, sweet, fruity ending to a meal. This mousse looks very pretty in parfait or tall wine glasses. They can be made a day ahead and decorated a couple of hours before serving.

Brandied Apple Mousse

PRALINE
¼ cup blanched almonds
⅓ cup sugar
2 tablespoons water

MOUSSE
3 Granny Smith apples
2 tablespoons butter
1 tablespoon apricot jam
2 tablespoons sugar
2 teaspoons gelatin
2 tablespoons lemon juice
1 whole egg
1 egg yolk
¼ cup sugar
2 tablespoons brandy
1½ cups whipping cream
3 tablespoons powdered sugar
½ teaspoon vanilla

1. Lightly grease a baking sheet with butter for the pralines.

2. With a knife, chop the almonds into small-ish pieces. Put the sugar and water into a small frying pan and bring to a boil over medium-high heat. Boil without stirring until it turns light brown. Quickly stir in the almonds, being careful not to burn the sugar mixture. Pour out onto the baking sheet and allow to cool. Once it has hardened, put it into a plastic bag and crush it with a meat pounder. Store in an airtight container.

MOUSSE

3. Peel and core the apples; slice thinly. In a medium frying pan over medium heat, melt the butter. Add the jam and 2 tablespoons sugar. Add the apples and stir. Cover and cook, stirring occasionally, until softened,

about 6 minutes. Put into the bowl of a food processor and puree. Pour into a medium bowl.

4. In a separate bowl, sprinkle the gelatin over the lemon juice and gently heat in the microwave to dissolve. Pour into the hot apple mixture. Using a double boiler, whisk together the egg, egg yolk and 1/4 cup sugar. Whisk over simmering water until it becomes slightly thickened. Do not cook it to scrambled eggs! Stir into the apple mixture, add the brandy and chill. Whip the cream with the powdered sugar and vanilla. Fold three-fourths of the cream into the apple mixture. Spoon into six individual dishes or tall wine glasses, decorate the top with the remaining cream and refrigerate.

5. Just before serving, sprinkle the top with some of the Pralines.

[SERVES 6]

Use a blend of chocolate, coffee and cinnamon to
make a rich ice cream that has the flavors of Mexican chocolate.

Mexican Chocolate Ice Cream

¾ pound good-quality semisweet
  chocolate

½ teaspoon instant espresso powder

2 cups whole milk

9 large egg yolks

1 cup sugar

1 tablespoon ground cinnamon

2 cups heavy cream, well chilled

2 teaspoons vanilla

1. Chop the chocolate into small pieces and put into a medium bowl along with the espresso powder. Put the milk into a medium saucepan and bring to a simmer. Heat just until small bubbles form around the side of the saucepan. Pour the hot milk over the chocolate and stir gently until the chocolate has melted.

2. Separate the eggs, being careful not to get any yolk in the bowl of whites. Freeze the egg whites in a plastic bag for making meringue in the future. In an electric mixer, beat the egg yolks with the sugar and cinnamon until they are creamy. Carefully whisk in the chocolate mixture. Pour the mixture into a clean, medium-sized saucepan and cook, stirring with a wooden spoon, over medium heat just until the mixture coats the back of the spoon or you see a little steam rising. You want to cook the egg yolks without turning them into scrambled eggs. Immediately pour the mixture into a bowl and add the chilled cream and vanilla. Cool the mixture down by placing in the fridge or put the bowl in a larger bowl you have half filled with ice and a little water; stir until quite cold.

3. Put into an ice cream machine and chill until frozen.

[SERVES 8]

We made this recipe for a big dinner party for the President of Rwanda.
It slices and looks like cheesecake but it is so light it is the perfect, refreshing
ending to a rich meal. Uncooked egg whites are generally safe to use.

Frozen Lemon Soufflé Cake with Strawberry Sauce

CRUST
½ (9-ounce) package chocolate wafer thins
3 tablespoons unsalted butter, melted

FILLING
⅔ cup sugar
3 tablespoons water
1¼ cups strained lemon juice, divided
4 egg whites, at room temperature
Pinch of salt
1¾ cups whipping cream, well chilled

4 tablespoons powdered sugar
Grated zest of 1 lemon

STRAWBERRY SAUCE
¼ cup sugar
¼ cup water
1 (10-ounce) bag frozen strawberries, thawed
1 teaspoon lemon juice

1. In a food processor, crumble the wafers and add the melted butter. Gently press into the bottom and a half inch up the sides of an 8-inch springform pan to form the crust; chill.

2. For the filling, combine the sugar and water in a medium saucepan. Add 1 tablespoon lemon juice. Over medium-high heat, boil until the mixture reaches soft-ball stage, 238 degrees F on a candy thermometer. Beat the egg whites with the salt until they have soft peaks. Continue beating while slowly pouring the sugar syrup into the egg whites in a steady stream. Beat until cooled, about 10 minutes.

3. In a chilled bowl, whip the cream with the powdered sugar. Fold the lemon juice into the egg white mixture along with the lemon zest.

Fold in the whipped cream. Spoon into the prepared shell. Freeze for at least 6 hours and up to 3 days.

4. Take out of the pan and allow to sit in the refrigerator for 10 minutes before serving.

5. Decorate with more whipped cream, lemon slices and sliced strawberries.

6. Serve with sauce drizzled on the plate.

7. For the sauce, dissolve the sugar in the water and bring to a boil. Boil for 2 minutes and pour into a bowl to cool slightly. In a food processor, puree the strawberries with the lemon juice and the sugar syrup. Strain through a fine strainer to get rid of the seeds. Drizzle on the serving plate in a design before topping with a slice of the frozen cake.

[SERVES 8]

Hazelnut and Raspberry Pavlova

1½ cups whole hazelnuts, divided

PAVLOVA

4 egg whites at room temperature

1 cup sugar

1 teaspoon white vinegar
1 teaspoon vanilla
1 tablespoon cornstarch

TOPPING

2 cups whipping cream

2 tablespoons powdered sugar
1 teaspoon vanilla
1 container fresh raspberries

1. Heat the oven to 375 degrees F. Put the hazelnuts on a baking sheet and place in the hot oven. At intervals shake the pan to move the hazelnuts around. Hazelnuts should be lightly brown with their skins a dark brown. Pour onto a tea towel, put another cloth on top and then roll them firmly with your hand to remove the skin. The skins will not totally come off. Put 1/2 cup of whole nuts into a food processor and grind finely. You will end up with 1/4 cup ground nuts.

2. Preheat the oven to 300 degrees F.

PAVLOVA

3. Beat the egg whites until they are stiff with an electric mixer. Slowly beat in the sugar with the mixer at medium-high speed. Turn the mixer to low and add the vinegar, vanilla and cornstarch. Fold in 1/4 cup ground

hazelnuts.

4. On a baking sheet lined with parchment paper, pile the egg white mixture into a 6-inch circle, smoothing the top and the sides as evenly as possible. Do not flatten as it will naturally do so as it cooks. Cook for 45 minutes, turn off the oven and allow to cool in the oven, about 2 hours or overnight. Carefully slide onto a serving plate.

TOPPING

5. For the topping, whip the cream with the powdered sugar and vanilla. Spread the top of the Pavlova with half the cream, put the rest in a piping bag and decorate with piped rosettes. Decorate with the raspberries and 1 cup whole hazelnuts. Decorate as close to serving as possible. The Pavlova will become chewy if refrigerated for longer than 3 hours.

[SERVES 8]

For this recipe you need a mini-cheesecake pan. The recipe can be made a week ahead and frozen if well wrapped. Take out of the freezer 10 minutes before serving to soften slightly and make unmolding easier.

Individual Frozen Lime Cheesecakes

CRUST
½ (9-ounce) box plain chocolate wafer cookies
4 tablespoons butter, melted

FILLING
1 (8-ounce) package cream cheese, at room temperature
¼ cup sugar
1½ tablespoons lime zest (3 to 4 limes)
2 tablespoons lime juice (2 limes)
1¼ cups whipping cream, whipped to soft peaks

TO DECORATE
1 cup whipping cream
1 tablespoon powdered sugar
½ teaspoon vanilla

CRUST
1. In a food processor, crush the cookies until they are crumbs. Add the melted butter and divide between 12 mini-cheesecake pans with removable bottoms (2-inch size). Press into the bottom. Or use one 7-inch cheese-cake pan.

FILLING
2. With an electric mixer beat the cream cheese and sugar together for the filling. Add the lime zest and juice. Gently fold in the whipped cream and fill the cheesecake pans. (It is easier to fill the small pans if you put the mixture into a piping bag with a large round tip.)

3. Freeze for at least 1 hour. If frozen for longer, take out of the freezer 10 minutes before serving to soften a little. Will freeze, covered, for up to 2 weeks.

TO DECORATE
4. Whip whipping cream with powdered sugar and vanilla. Put into a piping bag with a star tip.
5. Drizzle Strawberry Sauce (page 221) or Raspberry Sauce (page 226) on a plate in a pattern. Place 1 cheesecake in the center, pipe a swirl of cream onto the top of the cheesecake, decorate with a slice of lime and 2 fresh lime leaves.

[MAKES 12 MINI DESSERTS]

Praline Tacos

½ cup unsalted butter

½ cup sugar

½ cup golden syrup

½ cup all-purpose flour

1 teaspoon ground ginger

1. Preheat the oven to 350 degrees F.

2. In a medium saucepan over medium heat, melt together the butter, sugar and golden syrup. (Grease or oil the inside of a measuring cup before measuring the golden syrup and it will slip out easily.) Add the flour and ground ginger. Take off the heat.

3. Line a baking sheet with a silicone sheet liner. Using a teaspoon, put only 4 rounds of the batter on the baking sheet. They really spread out during cooking. Bake for about 10 minutes, or until they are bubbly and a medium golden brown. Take them out of the oven and allow them to sit until they cool off and set up enough so that you can get a spatula under them to take them off the sheet to

mold. If they set up too hard, put them back in the oven for a minute to soften.

4. To make taco shapes, put a rolling pin across a baking sheet and drape the cookie over the rolling pin to make a U shape.

5. To make bowls, turn a cupcake pan upside down and drape a cookie over the bottom of a cupcake mold. Press gently into a bowl shape.

6. Allow the cookies to cool and harden before taking them off the molds.

7. To serve, fill with small scoops of Mexican Chocolate Ice Cream (see page 220) or Chocolate-Chile Ice Cream (see page 214). Top with Poached Fruit Salsa (see page 208) and sprinkle with toasted coconut.

[MAKES 14 TACOS OR BOWLS]

Raspberry Sauce

1 (16-ounce) bag frozen raspberries

1 cup water

½ cup sugar

1 tablespoon lemon juice

1. In a saucepan, bring the raspberries, water, sugar and lemon juice to a boil. Reduce the heat and simmer for 10 minutes. Strain

through a fine strainer to remove the seeds. Chill in the refrigerator until needed.

[MAKES 2 CUPS]

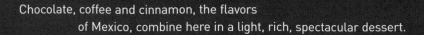

Chocolate, coffee and cinnamon, the flavors of Mexico, combine here in a light, rich, spectacular dessert.

Chilled Mexican Chocolate Soufflé

2 packages gelatin	1 teaspoon instant espresso powder	2 teaspoons vanilla
½ cup cold 2 percent milk		1 tablespoon Kahlua
1½ cups milk	6 large eggs, separated	2 cups heavy cream, well chilled
¾ pound semisweet chocolate	1 cup sugar	Additional whipped cream and
	1 tablespoon ground cinnamon	fresh berries to decorate

1. Put double parchment collars around ten 4-ounce soufflé dishes and hold in place with a rubber band.

2. Soften the gelatin in the 2 percent milk. Put the 1 1/2 cups of milk into a medium saucepan and bring to a simmer. Heat just until small bubbles form around the side of the saucepan.

3. Chop the chocolate into small pieces and put into a medium bowl along with the espresso powder. Add the hot milk and add the milk-gelatin mixture. Stir until the chocolate has melted.

4. Separate the eggs, being careful not to get any yolk in the bowl of whites. In an electric mixer, beat the egg yolks with the sugar and cinnamon until they are creamy. Carefully whisk in the chocolate mixture. Pour the mixture into a clean, medium-sized saucepan and cook, stirring with a wooden spoon, over medium heat just until the mixture coats the back of the spoon or you see a little steam rising. You want to cook the egg yolks without turning them into scrambled eggs.

5. Immediately pour the mixture into a cold bowl. Cool the mixture down by placing in the fridge or put the bowl in a larger bowl half filled with ice and a little water. Stir until quite cold and almost set. The mixture should resemble chocolate pudding. Stir in the vanilla and Kahlua. Whip the 2 cups chilled cream until thickened. With a clean beater, whip the egg whites until they form soft peaks. Gently fold the whipped cream into the chilled chocolate mixture, then fold in the egg whites and gently blend. Pour into the soufflé dishes, filling them above the top of the dish, about three-fourths of the way up the parchment collar. Allow to set in the refrigerator for at least 3 hours.

6. To serve, remove the parchment collar and decorate with additional whipped cream and fresh berries.

HINT: This can be made into 1 large soufflé or 10 individual soufflés. Cut pieces of parchment or wax paper long enough to wrap around the ramekins and stand about 2 inches above the rim of the dish. Secure with a rubber band. This allows you to fill the soufflé above the rim of the dish, which makes a great presentation once the collar is removed for serving.

[SERVES 10]

For this recipe you need a sweet bread, like challah or brioche. If you cannot find a sweet bread, you can use plain white bread. The caramel sauce can also be flavored with bourbon or brandy.

Banana-White Chocolate Bread Pudding with Caramel-Rum Sauce

1½ tablespoons unsalted butter
¼ cup sugar
2 medium bananas, peeled and sliced
½ teaspoon cinnamon
2 large eggs
½ cup sugar

¾ teaspoon vanilla
1¾ cups whipping cream
1 tablespoon rum
½ cup golden raisins
1 loaf of challah or brioche bread, sliced about ½ inch thick
4 ounces good white chocolate, chopped

CARAMEL-RUM SAUCE
6 tablespoons unsalted butter
½ cup light corn syrup
1 cup sugar
1½ cups whipping cream, heated in the microwave.
3 tablespoons dark rum

1. Preheat oven to 350 degrees F.
2. Melt the butter in a large frying pan over medium-high heat. Add the 1/4 cup sugar and cook until lightly browned. Add the bananas and cinnamon and cook for about 2 minutes or until soft and caramelized. Pour into a bowl and mash with a potato masher.
3. With an electric mixer, beat the eggs and the 1/2 cup sugar until creamy. Add the vanilla.
4. In a saucepan, heat the cream until it is hot. Slowly and carefully pour into the egg mixture. Stir in the mashed bananas. Pour the rum over the raisins.
5. Line a buttered 9 x 13-inch glass baking dish with slices of the bread, pour half the egg-banana mixture over the bread, sprinkle with half the white chocolate and all the rum-soaked raisins. Top with more bread (you may not need the whole loaf), banana-egg mixture

and white chocolate. Allow to sit for an hour for the bread to absorb the liquids. Bake for about 40 minutes, or until the pudding is puffed and brown and a toothpick comes out clean. Serve warm with the sauce.

CARAMEL-RUM SAUCE

6. For the sauce, melt the butter in a heavy, medium-sized frying pan with the corn syrup and sugar. Cook over medium-high heat, without stirring until it turns a light caramel color. When the edges begin to color, gently move the mixture around with a wooden spoon so it browns evenly. Take off the heat and slowly add the cream, stirring. The sauce will lump so put it back over low heat until the lumps have dissolved. Take off the heat and pour into a serving dish. Stir in the rum.

[SERVES 8]

Index